The Complete Book of Salads

Created and
designed by the
editorial staff of
ORTHO Books

Written by
Cynthia Scheer

Designed by
James Stockton

Photography by
Fred Lyon

Photo Styling by
Sara Slavin

Illustrations by
Ellen Blonder

Ortho Books

Publisher
Robert L. Iacopi

Editorial Director
Min S. Yee

Managing Editor
Anne Coolman

Horticultural Editor
Michael D. Smith

Senior Editor
Kenneth R. Burke

Production Manager
Laurie S. Blackman

Horticulturist
Michael McKinley

Associate Editors
Barbara J. Ferguson
Susan M. Lammers

Administrative Assistant
Judith C. Pillon

Production Assistant
Anne D. Pederson

Editorial Assistant
Julie W. Hall

Copyediting by
Editcetera
Berkeley, CA

Typography by
Sigmagraph, Inc.
San Francisco, CA

Color Separations by
Colorscan
Palo Alto, CA

Address all inquiries to:
Ortho Books
Chevron Chemical Company
Consumer Products Division
575 Market Street
San Francisco, CA 94105

Special thanks to:

Oakville Grocery
San Francisco, CA

The Red Pony
Portola Valley, CA
(custom-made hutch, page 88)

Printed in August, 1981
1 2 3 4 5 6 7 8 9 10

ISBN 0-917102-96-7

Library of Congress Catalog Card
Number 80-85219

Front Cover Photograph:
With crisp greens and fresh vegetables you can make an infinite
variety of mouth-watering salads.
Recipes begin on page 11.

Page 1 Photograph:
Home Economist/Writer Cynthia
Scheer shops for salad ingredients.

Back Cover Photographs:
A sampling of the delicious salads
that await you.
Upper left Red Fruit Plate with
Cream Cheese Dressing, page 47
Upper right Chicken Salad with Ap-
ricots and Avocados, page 67
Lower left Creamy Blueberry Salad,
page 33
Lower right Red-and-White Potato
Salad, page 52

The Complete Book of Salads

All About Salads

I f ever there was an anything-goes kind of food, an eat-it-anytime food, an uninhibited sort of food, its name is *salad*.

With all that delicious freedom, it isn't easy to define a salad. People enjoy them as appetizers, first courses, accompaniments to dinner, refreshers following a main course, whole meals, and even desserts. Most salads are cold, but some of the best are hot.

The majority contain some lettuce. Greengrocers say we are eating more lettuce than ever before—per capita consumption has more than doubled in 30 years. It is a safe bet that most of it goes into salads.

One could hardly argue, however, that lettuce is a compulsory salad ingredient. An inventive spirit can create a salad from virtually anything edible. Improved varieties of produce that tolerate marginal weather, and modern shipping methods, guarantee a host of salad makings for all seasons.

What salads of all kinds have in common is an appeal to each of the senses. They look beautiful, taste great, and fill the air with irresistible aromas. They also make good nutritional sense. Just looking at such typical salad components as crisp, dewy greens and juicy citrus fruits gives a person a healthy feeling. Feasting on them is even better!

This book is an exploration of the pleasures of salads of every sort. You will find recipes for old favorites, salads from many regions and cuisines, ideas from today's inventive salad-makers, and suggestions to inspire your own creativity with the salad bowl.

Salads to Suit Every Occasion

The most familiar kind of salad is a green one, leafy and refreshing. It is versatile enough to serve before, with, or after the main course. A close relative is the marinated vegetable salad, made with either cooked or raw vegetables. Salads of this sort can be interesting first courses or elements of main dish salad plates.

Fruit salads are also dependably pleasing. Count on them to enhance a meal with their rich colors and natural sweetness.

Cooks who like to plan ahead count on molded gelatin salads. Their shimmering shapes add eye appeal to many a buffet supper, and when served in individual portions, they make handsome first courses.

The salads everyone thinks of for picnics and barbecues are substantial —salads with potatoes, rice, pasta, or beans. Imagine fried chicken without potato salad! Innovate with salads of this sort.

With the current emphasis on lighter eating, salads have grown in popularity as main dishes. Hot or cold or served sandwich-style, a salad may be your favorite full meal.

Almost any food can be a part of an enticing salad—vegetables, fruits, pasta, potatoes, meats, cheese, herbs. The crisp watercress and fresh mushroom salad (right) previews ideas to come.

🍂 Greens: The Beginning of Great Salads

Because greens are such a fundamental part of most salads, this is a good place to look at the most common market and garden varieties.

■ *Iceberg lettuce* is the salad green that probably comes most readily to mind when you think of lettuce. The compact, round, smooth heads are made up of crisp, pale, bland-tasting leaves. It is hard to imagine Mexican dishes such as tostadas, for example, without shredded iceberg lettuce. But for variety in your salad bowl, try some other greens.

■ *Romaine or cos lettuce* takes the form of long, narrow, rather dark green leaves in an almost loaf-shaped head. Dependably crisp, this is the lettuce favored for the classic Caesar salad, and it is also good in combination with softer-leafed lettuce.

■ *Butter or Boston lettuce* consists of small, fluffily rounded heads of soft, medium-green leaves. Close relatives are *Bibb and limestone lettuce*, rarely seen in retail stores except those dealing in luxury produce; both are known for their gossamer crispness and delicate flavor. This type of lettuce, simply dressed with oil and vinegar, makes up the refreshing salad that follows the main course of a French dinner.

■ *Leaf lettuces* include the ruffly varieties that, whether grown commercially or in your own garden, never really form heads. *Red leaf lettuce* with its red-bronze edges contrasts nicely with other greens; *green leaf lettuce* lines salad plates and tastes good in sandwiches; *Australian lettuce* has handsome, long, scalloped, medium-green leaves.

■ *Endive* is the name of a whole family of assertively flavored salad bowl participants. *Belgian endive* is the most elegant — and costly — member. The small, pale, pointy heads are mostly imported; their tender-crisp leaves have a distinctly bitter flavor. *Chicory or curly endive* has large, curly, feathery leaves and a similarly bitter taste. *Escarole* is a broad, flat-leafed endive with long, dark green leaves; popular in Italian cooking, this green adds texture and bite to a mixed salad.

■ *Watercress* is usually used as an accent or garnish — it has a peppery flavor stronger than the size of its little round leaves would lead you to expect. It can make a dramatic statement, however, in a first-course salad in combination with just one other element — sliced raw mushrooms, for example.

■ *Arugula or rocket* takes the form of small, slender, notched, dark green leaves. It has a bittersweet, almost nutlike flavor that may take some getting used to. It is probably best used as an accent unless you are sure of your diners' preferences. A member of the mustard family, it is another Italian favorite, bathed in olive oil and red wine vinegar.

■ *Sprouts* that are generally available in supermarket produce departments are wispy *alfalfa sprouts* and pale, tender *bean sprouts*. But if you appreciate their ethereal texture and distinctive flavors — *radish sprouts*, for instance, have a surprising bite — sprouts are easy to grow in your own kitchen from seeds purchased at a garden or health food store (page 21).

■ *Cabbage* always seems to be available, no matter how grim the weather or remote the grocery store. In addition to the familiar *green cabbage,* you can add variety to cabbage salads with *red cabbage,* crinkly-leafed *Savoy or curly cabbage,* and long, crisp *Chinese cabbage* (also known as *Napa or celery cabbage*).

■ *Spinach* is more appealing to many people in its pristine state than cooked. Several varieties are available: one kind with smooth, tapered leaves; another with rounder, crumpled-looking leaves; and a third (known as New Zealand spinach) that has thicker leaves and is neither spinach nor from New Zealand. They can be used interchangeably in salads.

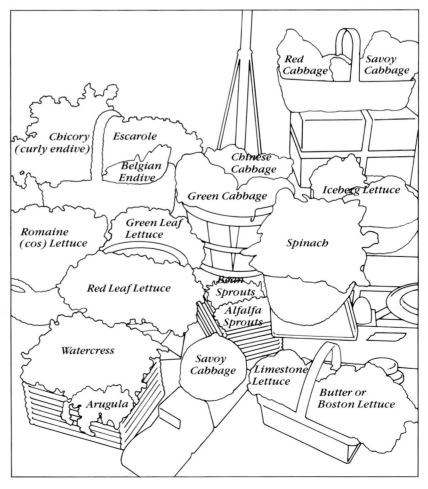

Greens of all sorts are a fundamental ingredient of many salads. They are identified in the drawing at the right.

Watercress stays fresh in the refrigerator when placed upright in water.

🌱 Selection and Care of Salad Greens

Choosing the best greens doesn't require great skill. Look for crisp, clean greens free of brown spots. Most are sold by the head or bunch, but occasionally you will find them priced by the pound. In a way, selling lettuce by weight makes sense—the heavier the head, the more leaves it contains.

When you bring greens home, rinse them well, discarding any discolored or badly wilted outer leaves. Iceberg lettuce and cabbage can simply be rinsed under cold water. To cleanse looser heads or bunches of greens and spinach of grit, remove the core (if any), separate leaves slightly, and dunk them up and down in a deep basin of very cold water. Let them soak for a few minutes; leaves will float to the top while particles of dirt sink.

After washing, invert greens and drain well in a colander, lettuce basket, or salad spinner. Wrap them in a clean kitchen towel or paper towels and refrigerate until crisp and dry, 1 to 2 hours. Now the greens are ready for salad-making.

If you don't plan to use greens right away, place them in a plastic bag or a covered refrigerator container and store them in a cold, moist part of the refrigerator. In some types of refrigerators, evaporation from unwrapped greens can be quite rapid, so it's important to store them properly.

Watercress keeps best in the refrigerator if you treat it as a bouquet. After rinsing and draining, stand the stems of the watercress in a tumbler or other deep, narrow container in about 4 inches of water. Cover the leaves loosely with a plastic bag. This way, watercress will stay fresh and ready to use for several days. The same technique works for fresh herbs, such as cilantro (fresh coriander or Chinese parsley) and basil, usually sold by the bunch.

If you place greens with other vegetables in a produce drawer in the refrigerator, be sure they are not in the same bin as apples, pears, plums, melons, tomatoes, or avocados. These can cause greens to develop brownish spots.

The sooner you use greens after buying them, the better. However, a useful generality is that the softer the lettuce, the shorter the time it can be kept in good condition. For example, romaine lasts longer than butter or leaf lettuce.

🌱 Tools of the Salad Trade

Actually, you don't need any special equipment to make good salads. Many aids are available, however, and some can be quite useful.

When you prepare greens and other salad vegetables, an ample colander is helpful. Salad spinners are a recent and deservedly popular development. Operating on the principle of centrifugal force, they contain a rotating central basket in which lettuce or other greens are placed. When you turn the handle, this basket whirls the lettuce, spinning out much of the moisture.

Select a salad spinner large enough to hold the types of lettuce or other greens you prefer. After greens have been spun in one of these devices, they still need a certain amount of blotting to be dry enough to make a good salad. Don't assume lettuce can go straight from the spinner into the salad bowl.

The collapsible lettuce basket is a homey-looking piece of equipment that works in a similar way. But—it must be whirled outdoors since it is not self-contained and releases a spray of water. Twirling your greens basket in the garden on a nice day is one of the small pleasures of salad-making.

For cutting up certain salad ingredients, good knives are essential. Kitchen scissors are useful for snipping chives and parsley. A food processor with its variety of cutting blades shreds carrots or thinly slices cucumbers with lightning efficiency. However, unless you make salads day after day for a mob, you may feel you can make do with a French chef's knife, a paring knife, a vegetable peeler, and a stainless steel four-sided grater.

Once assembled, most salads are so handsome it is a pleasure to bring them to the table to be admired and devoured. Present them in a large serving bowl, on an attractive platter, or as individual servings.

At one time a certain mystique surrounded wooden salad bowls, but serving salads strictly in wood appears to be on the wane nowadays. Good-looking glass and ceramic bowls are quite common, and they can be washed sparkling clean so that unpleasant flavors don't intrude on subsequent salads.

If you use wooden salad bowls, for goodness sake, *do* wash them. Otherwise oils collect in their porous surfaces and create off flavors. Soaking a wooden bowl may warp or crack it, but a brief, thorough washing in warm, sudsy water will not be harmful if you rinse and dry the bowl quickly.

For a leafy green salad, a broad, shallow bowl allows ample room for mixing and keeps greens from packing down and becoming crushed. Wooden salad servers are attractive, but two large spoons work just as well for mixing and serving.

What About Wine with Salad?

Wine writers sometimes give the impression that wine and salad *never* mix. When one considers the enormous diversity of salads, it is hard to believe that the two cannot sometimes be successfully paired.

The reason wine buffs hesitate to serve wine with salad is that most salads are dressed with a sharply acid-flavored mixture—either vinegar or lemon juice—that can obscure the delicate flavor of many wines.

That does not mean that certain salads cannot be accompanied by carefully selected wines. A fruit salad with a creamy dressing may be quite pleasant with a chilled, fruity white wine such as Chenin Blanc. Many people enjoy a hearty red jug wine or a young Gamay Beaujolais with a robust blue cheese–dressed green salad. In the south of France, an olive oil–drenched *salade Niçoise* tastes wonderful with a dry rosé of that region. Perfectly ripe sliced tomatoes drizzled with the *pesto* of Genoa are in good company with crusty bread and an unpretentious red wine.

Throughout this book, suggestions for wines are made where appropriate. When you pair wine and salad, always select flavors that will enhance, not conflict with, each other.

Green salad with a creamy blue cheese dressing is enjoyable with a young, unpretentious red wine before or after the main course of a dinner.

Green and Vegetable Salads

The word *salad* evokes images of greens—ruffled lettuces and a rainbow of vegetables worthy of Mr. McGregor's garden. Surely a leafy green salad glistening with a skillful oil-and-vinegar dressing is one of the most refreshing dishes imaginable.

Inspired salad-makers know that lettuce and tomatoes are only the beginning of great salads. Choosing from a variety of greens, cooked and raw vegetables, crisp accents, and flavorful dressings leads to endless possible combinations.

Flavor is the first consideration when combining salad elements. Some lettuces—iceberg, butter or Boston, leaf—have mild flavors that mix effectively with more assertive types such as watercress, spinach, arugula, and members of the endive family.

Another quality esteemed in salads is crisp *texture*. One counts on salad for contrast with tender foods such as noodles or meat loaf. If a salad is mainly a soft-leafed lettuce, it can probably benefit from the addition of crisper romaine—or slivers of crunchy radish, red or green pepper, or cucumber.

Appearance also counts in salad-making. Contrast pale greens with darker ones, then add colorful elements discreetly: dots of orange in the form of thinly sliced carrot, red cherry tomato orbs, or purple cabbage shreds. Learn to turn out a few simple vegetable garnishes. Cut thin slices of cucumber or tomato, or lime, lemon, or orange; cut each slice just to the center, then give it a jaunty twist. Using a vegetable peeler, cut long thin strips of carrot; wrap each into about a 1-inch-diameter curl and fasten with a wooden pick, then crisp in ice water. Sliver ends of 2-inch-long celery sticks to make fans; chill in ice water.

Leafy Green Salads

The basic salad ingredient, lettuce, tastes and looks best if treated carefully between market and table. Follow the washing and storing recommendations for greens on page 8. A mixed green salad will taste best if the greens are crisp, well dried, and cold before you add dressing. If greens are too wet, dressing will not cling to them, and its flavor will be diluted.

Greens and garden vegetables make some of the most refreshing salads. Cabbage-shaped bowl in center holds Fruited Cabbage Salad (the recipe appears on page 19). At right, perfect leaves of crisp romaine glisten with homemade dressing.

How much can you do ahead? Greens can be torn, placed in a plastic bag or the bowl in which the salad will be mixed, covered, and refrigerated several hours in advance. The dressing can also be made. An oil-and-vinegar dressing can wait at room temperature for several hours, but a creamy one should be covered and refrigerated if made ahead.

With the exception of shredded lettuce and cabbage for certain salads, greens will be most pleasing if *torn* rather than cut. In this country lettuce is usually served in bite-size pieces in a salad — although in France, the most familiar salad is made with whole leaves of butter lettuce (which are folded with the fork, never cut, to eat).

Mix the salad at the last possible moment before serving it. You might even do this at the table for a touch of showmanship. The reason? Dressing tends to make lettuce limp as a salad stands.

The phrase *tossed salad* is a bit misleading, because greens should be handled gently. When you mix a salad, use two large spoons or a pair of salad servers and a light, up-and-over motion — rather like folding egg whites into a soufflé or angel food cake batter.

Figure on about 2 quarts (8 cups) of lightly packed greens for 4 servings of a mixed salad. For this quantity of lettuce, you will need about 1/3 cup of an oil-and-vinegar dressing or 1/3 to 1/2 cup of a creamy one. Too much dressing will overwhelm the greens, but too little will leave them tasteless and uninteresting.

Show-Off Green Salad resembles a Caesar salad in the drama of its preparation.

Show-Off Green Salad

Fresh mint accents this prepared-at-the-table salad. Some of the ingredients and the sequence of combining them may remind you of a Caesar salad, but this one includes several things never found in that classic.

1 egg
    Boiling water
8 cups torn romaine
3 green onions, thinly sliced
1 large tomato, cut in small wedges
6 slices bacon, crisply cooked, drained, and crumbled
3 tablespoons lemon juice
2 teaspoons chopped fresh mint leaves (or ½ teaspoon dried mint)
¼ teaspoon dried oregano
⅛ teaspoon salt
⅓ cup olive oil
    Freshly ground black pepper
⅓ cup freshly grated Parmesan cheese
1 cup Garlic Croutons (see page 26)

1. Place egg on a spoon and carefully lower it into a small pan of boiling water. Immediately remove pan from heat; let egg stand in water 1 minute. Remove egg and place in cold water.
2. In a large salad bowl, place (in order given) romaine, green onions, tomato wedges, and crumbled bacon.
3. In a medium bowl, mix lemon juice, mint, oregano, and salt; using a whisk or fork, gradually beat in oil.
4. Bring to table the egg, salad bowl, dressing, pepper mill, cheese, and croutons. Grind pepper generously over greens. Mix gently with dressing. Break in prepared egg and mix well. Sprinkle with cheese and croutons and mix again. Serve at once.

Makes 4 servings.

Caesar Salad

Here is that classic, said to have been created by a hotel chef in Baja California in the 1920s. Some versions merely rub the serving bowl with garlic, but using it in the dressing gives a more pronounced flavor. Adorning the salad with your own homemade croutons (recipes, page 26) adds something special.

1 egg
    Boiling water
8 cups torn romaine
3 tablespoons lemon juice
1 clove garlic, minced or pressed
1 teaspoon Dijon mustard
⅓ cup olive oil
6 flat anchovy fillets, drained, finely chopped
    Freshly ground black pepper
⅓ cup freshly grated Parmesan cheese
1 cup Garlic, Parmesan, *or* Herbed Croutons (see page 26)

1. Place egg on a spoon and carefully lower it into a small pan of boiling water. Immediately remove pan from heat; let egg stand in water 1 minute. Remove egg and place in cold water.
2. In a large salad bowl place romaine; if done ahead, cover and refrigerate.
3. In a medium bowl mix lemon juice, garlic, and mustard. Using a whisk or fork, gradually beat in oil. Mix in anchovies.
4. Bring to table the egg, salad bowl, dressing, pepper mill, cheese, and croutons. Grind pepper generously over greens. Mix gently with dressing. Break in prepared egg and mix well. Sprinkle with cheese and croutons and mix again. Serve at once.

Makes 4 servings.

Mendocino Garden Salad

This salad looks particularly perky as a first course or on a buffet.

8 cups torn green leaf lettuce
½ medium cucumber, grooved and thinly sliced (see page 17)
1 cup shredded red cabbage
    Garlic-Red Wine Vinegar Dressing (recipe follows)

4 green onions, thinly slivered
   lengthwise (see page 17)
½ cup slivered sweet red or green
   bell pepper

1. In a salad bowl lightly mix lettuce, cucumber, and red cabbage.
2. Mix lightly with dressing.
3. Top with slivered onions and red
pepper.
Makes 4 to 6 servings.

Garlic-Red Wine Vinegar Dressing
In a medium bowl mix 2 tablespoons red wine vinegar, 1 teaspoon
Dijon mustard, 1 clove garlic
(minced or pressed), ¼ teaspoon
dried marjoram, ⅛ teaspoon salt,
and a dash of seasoned pepper. Using
a whisk or fork, gradually mix in 2
tablespoons olive oil and ¼ cup
salad oil until well blended and
slightly thickened. Makes about ⅓
cup.

Salad Fabbro

This simple salad of romaine and
shredded cheese is a showcase for one
of the most elegant of all vinegars—
fragrant, aged balsamic vinegar,
imported from Italy. Lacking it, you
might substitute sherry wine vinegar or red wine vinegar.

1 head romaine, torn into
   bite-size pieces (7 to 8 cups)
1½ tablespoons balsamic vinegar
1 small clove garlic, minced or
   pressed
⅛ teaspoon salt
¼ cup olive oil
⅓ cup coarsely shredded
   fontinella, kasseri, or Parmesan
   cheese
   Freshly ground black pepper

1. Place romaine in salad bowl.
2. In small bowl mix vinegar, garlic, and salt. Using a whisk or fork,
gradually beat in olive oil until well
blended.
3. Mix dressing and cheese lightly
with romaine. Grind pepper over
each serving to taste.
Makes 4 servings.

Smoked oysters and crispy homemade croutons accent this salad.

Smoked Oyster Green Salad
Combining the features of a green
salad and a light seafood dish, this
salad makes an excellent first course.
The oysters add a smoky flavor.

6 cups torn green leaf lettuce
4 cups torn romaine
1 cup halved cherry tomatoes
   Garlic Vinaigrette Dressing
   (recipe follows)
1 can (3½ to 4 oz) smoked oysters,
   well drained
1 cup Parmesan Croutons
   (see page 26)

1. In a large salad bowl mix lettuce,
romaine, and cherry tomatoes.
2. Mix lightly with dressing.
Sprinkle evenly with smoked oysters
and croutons.
Makes 6 servings.

Garlic Vinaigrette Dressing
In a medium bowl mix 2 tablespoons red wine vinegar, ½ tablespoon lemon juice, 2 teaspoons
Dijon mustard, 1 clove garlic
(minced or pressed), ¼ teaspoon
salt, and a dash of coarsely ground
black pepper. Using a whisk or fork,
gradually blend in 2 tablespoons
olive oil and ⅓ cup salad oil, mixing until well blended and slightly
thickened. Stir in 1 tablespoon
chopped fresh parsley. Makes about
½ cup.

Dilled Lettuce and Mushroom Salad

A creamy dill-flavored dressing and
a finishing touch of crunchy sunflower seeds are the distinctive features of this lettuce, tomato, and
mushroom salad.

10 cups torn romaine or iceberg
   lettuce
½ pound mushrooms, thinly sliced
   Creamy Dill Dressing (recipe
   follows)
1 medium tomato, cut in wedges
¼ cup roasted sunflower seeds

1. In a large salad bowl combine lettuce and mushrooms.
2. Add dressing and mix lightly.
3. Arrange tomato wedges around
edge. Sprinkle sunflower seeds in
center.
Makes 6 servings.

Creamy Dill Dressing
In a medium bowl mix ½ cup mayonnaise, 1 teaspoon dried dill weed,
1 tablespoon lemon juice, 2 teaspoons white wine vinegar, and
1 teaspoon Dijon mustard. Using
a whisk or fork, gradually beat in
3 tablespoons salad oil. Makes about
¾ cup.

Red Pepper, Mushroom, and Garbanzo Salad

If you are serving a baked pasta main dish for a buffet supper, this colorful and substantial salad is a delightful accompaniment.

1 head romaine, torn into bite-size pieces (7 to 8 cups)
¼ pound mushrooms, thinly sliced
1 sweet red bell pepper, quartered, seeded, and cut in thin strips
1 small can (8¾ oz) garbanzo beans, drained (see note)
  Creamy Vinaigrette Dressing (recipe follows)
2 tablespoons freshly shredded Parmesan cheese
2 ounces thinly sliced dry salami, slivered
½ cup diced Swiss cheese (about ¼-in. cubes)

1. In a large salad bowl lightly mix romaine, mushrooms, red pepper, and beans. (Cover and refrigerate if made ahead.)
2. Just before serving lightly mix in dressing, then Parmesan cheese. Sprinkle with salami and Swiss cheese.
Makes 8 servings.

Creamy Vinaigrette Dressing
In a medium bowl mix 1 egg yolk, 2 tablespoons red wine vinegar, 1 tablespoon Dijon mustard, 1 clove garlic (minced or pressed), ½ teaspoon salt, and ⅛ teaspoon pepper until well combined. Using a whisk or fork, gradually beat in ⅓ cup *each* olive oil and salad oil until dressing is slightly thickened and creamy. Makes just under 1 cup.
Note: Garbanzo beans are also known as ceci beans or chick peas.

Bacon, Lettuce, and Tomato Salad with Blue Cheese

Here is a big, good-looking salad that brings together many favorite foods.

¼ cup *each* olive oil and salad oil
2 tablespoons sherry wine vinegar
1 tablespoon lemon juice
¼ teaspoon *each* salt and paprika
1 teaspoon Dijon mustard
½ teaspoon Worcestershire sauce
1 small clove garlic
¾ cup crumbled blue-veined cheese
6 cups *each* torn romaine and leaf lettuce
1 tomato, cut in wedges
5 slices bacon, crisply cooked, drained, and crumbled
2 hard-cooked eggs, grated
  Freshly ground black pepper

1. In blender or food processor combine oils, vinegar, lemon juice, salt, paprika, mustard, Worcestershire sauce, garlic, and ½ cup of the cheese. Whirl or process until smooth.
2. Combine lettuces in a large salad bowl. Mix lightly with dressing.
3. Garnish with tomato wedges, crumbled bacon, grated eggs, and remaining ¼ cup cheese. Grind pepper over each serving to taste.
Makes 6 to 8 servings.

Sprouts and Water Chestnut Salad

Use either mung or azuki bean sprouts—from a produce market or your own sprouter (see page 21)—to make this healthy salad. The curried yogurt dressing has an eye-opening zing!

4 cups (about ½ lb) fresh bean sprouts
1 can (8½ oz) water chestnuts, drained and thinly sliced
½ cup thinly sliced celery
½ cup slivered green onions (see page 17)
2 tablespoons chopped fresh cilantro (Chinese parsley) *or* parsley
  Curried Yogurt Dressing (recipe follows)
  Red leaf lettuce
¼ cup chopped dry-roasted cashews

1. In a medium bowl combine bean sprouts, water chestnuts, celery, green onions, and cilantro.
2. Mix lightly with dressing.
3. Serve in a lettuce-lined bowl or on lettuce leaves on individual plates. Sprinkle with cashews.
Makes 4 servings.

Curried Yogurt Dressing
Smoothly mix ⅓ cup mayonnaise, ¼ cup plain yogurt, 1 small clove garlic (minced or pressed), 1 teaspoon soy sauce, ½ teaspoon curry powder, ¼ teaspoon salt, and a dash of cayenne pepper. Makes about ⅔ cup.

Watercress and Mushroom Salad

The singular texture of sliced fresh mushrooms contrasts nicely with sprigs of watercress in a mustard-and-tarragon–flavored dressing. This salad is an elegant introduction to a multi-course dinner.

1 bunch watercress (about 6 oz)
½ pound mushrooms, thinly sliced
1 tablespoon *each* red wine vinegar and lemon juice
1 shallot, finely chopped, or 1 tablespoon finely chopped mild red onion
1 tablespoon Dijon mustard
¼ teaspoon *each* salt and sugar
⅛ teaspoon dried tarragon
  Dash white pepper
1 tablespoon olive oil
¼ cup salad oil
1 tablespoon *each* chopped fresh parsley and snipped chives (optional)

1. Remove leaves from watercress, using only tender stems; discard coarse stems. You should have about 3 cups leaves and stems. Combine with mushrooms in a medium bowl. If done ahead, cover and refrigerate.
2. For dressing, in a small bowl mix vinegar, lemon juice, shallot, mustard, salt, sugar, tarragon, and pepper. Using a whisk or fork, gradually beat in olive oil and salad oil until slightly thickened and well combined. Mix in parsley and chives.
3. Mix dressing lightly with watercress mixture. Serve at once.
Makes 4 to 6 servings.

First-course salads, clockwise from top left: Green Salad with Walnuts and Oranges (page 16), Belgian Endive Salad with Beets, Watercress and Mushroom Salad, and Avocado Salad Plate.

Avocado Salad Plate with Basil Dressing

An avocado half makes an appetizing container for a pristine oil-and-vinegar dressing. The better the quality of the olive oil, the more interesting the flavor of the salad.

1   avocado, halved, peeled, and seeded (see page 24)
    Butter or Boston lettuce
1   small tomato, sliced
    Basil Dressing (recipe follows)
½   cup alfalfa sprouts (see page 21)
1   green onion, thinly sliced
2   tablespoons roasted sunflower seeds

1. Place avocado half, on a lettuce leaf, on each of 2 salad plates. Arrange tomato slices beside avocado. Drizzle basil dressing lightly over avocado and tomatoes; spoon any remaining dressing into hollow of avocado.
2. Sprinkle tomatoes with alfalfa sprouts, green onion, and finally sunflower seeds. Serve at once.

Makes 2 servings.

Basil Dressing

In a small bowl mix 1 tablespoon sherry wine vinegar or red wine vinegar, 1 teaspoon lemon juice, ¼ teaspoon salt, a dash *each* sugar and coarsely ground black pepper, and 2 teaspoons chopped fresh basil (or ½ teaspoon dried basil). Using a whisk or fork, gradually beat in 3 tablespoons olive oil until well combined. Makes about ¼ cup.

Belgian Endive Salad with Beets

An unusual spiced vinaigrette dressing flavors this classic salad combination. If you prefer a more conventional dressing, the mustard vinaigrette for the watercress salad on page 14 is also a pleasing complement.

1   small can (8¼ oz) julienne beets, well drained
    Spicy Vinaigrette Dressing (recipe follows)
    Butter or Boston lettuce
½   pound Belgian endive
1   hard-cooked egg, shredded

1. Mix beets with half the dressing. Cover and refrigerate for ½ hour or longer to blend flavors.
2. To serve, on a butter lettuce leaf on each of 4 salad plates arrange endive leaves in a sunburst. Place a spoonful of beets with dressing in center of each, using a fourth of the beet mixture for each portion.
3. Stir or beat remaining dressing to mix well. Drizzle evenly over salads. Sprinkle with shredded egg.

Makes 4 servings.

Spicy Vinaigrette Dressing

In a small bowl mix 1 tablespoon *each* lime or lemon juice and peach wine vinegar or white wine vinegar, 1 teaspoon Dijon mustard, ¼ teaspoon *each* salt and paprika, and ⅛ teaspoon *each* ground cloves and cardamom. Using a whisk or fork, gradually beat in 1 tablespoon walnut oil or olive oil and ¼ cup salad oil, mixing until smooth and slightly thickened. Makes about 6 tablespoons.

Yogurt dressing complements Spinach and Garden Vegetable Salad, its crisp elements shown in layers before mixing.

Tangy Yogurt Dressing

Mix ⅔ cup plain yogurt, ⅓ cup mayonnaise, and 2 teaspoons Dijon mustard until smooth and well combined. Mix in 3 green onions (thinly sliced) and 1 clove garlic (minced or pressed). Cover and refrigerate for 1 hour or longer to blend flavors. Makes about 1 cup.

Aegean Salad

This leafy salad is refreshing before, with, or following a Greek-style main course. During warm weather it can also serve as a main dish for 2 or 3 people, simply by doubling the amount of cheese.

    Oregano Dressing (recipe follows)
½ cup moist Greek olives
4 cups *each* torn red and green leaf lettuce
½ cup slivered mild red onion
1 medium tomato, chopped
1 small green pepper, seeded and slivered
½ cup crumbled feta cheese

1. Pour dressing over olives in a small bowl; cover and let stand for at least 30 minutes at room temperature.
2. In a salad bowl combine lettuce, onion, tomato, and green pepper. Mix lightly with olives and dressing.
3. Sprinkle with cheese.

Makes 4 to 6 servings.

Oregano Dressing

In a small bowl mix 1 tablespoon red wine vinegar, 2 teaspoons lemon juice, 1 clove garlic (minced or pressed), ½ teaspoon *each* salt and dried oregano, and ⅛ teaspoon coarsely ground pepper. Using a whisk or fork, gradually beat in ¼ cup olive oil until well blended. Makes about ⅓ cup.

Green Salad with Walnuts and Oranges

This salad is lovely either before or after a dinner of roast pork or duckling.

8 cups torn romaine leaves
4 cups bite-size torn chicory
4 green onions, thinly sliced
2 oranges, peeled, sliced into rounds, then halved
    Walnut Oil Dressing (recipe follows)
⅓ cup coarsely chopped toasted walnuts

1. In a large bowl gently mix greens, onions, and oranges.
2. Mix lightly with dressing. Sprinkle with nuts.

Makes 6 to 8 servings.

Walnut Oil Dressing

In a medium bowl mix 2 tablespoons white wine vinegar or tarragon wine vinegar, 1 teaspoon lemon juice, 2 teaspoons Dijon mustard, ¼ teaspoon salt, and ⅛ teaspoon white pepper. Using a whisk or fork, gradually mix in 3 tablespoons walnut oil and ⅓ cup salad oil until well blended and slightly thickened. Makes about ⅔ cup.

Spinach and Garden Vegetable Salad

The amounts given in this recipe will make a first-course salad for 4 to 6 or a vegetarian main dish (nice for lunch or supper on a hot day with whole-grain bread) for 2 or 3.

1 bunch (about ¾ lb) spinach
6 ounces mushrooms, sliced
2 medium carrots, thinly sliced
1 cup halved cherry tomatoes
2 cups alfalfa or mixed sprouts (see page 21)
½ medium cucumber, thinly sliced
    Tangy Yogurt Dressing (recipe follows)
¼ cup roasted sunflower seeds
    Radish roses, for garnish (see page 65)

1. Remove and discard stems from spinach. (You should have about 6 cups leaves.)
2. In a salad bowl combine spinach, mushrooms, carrots, tomatoes, sprouts, and cucumber. Add dressing and mix lightly; or, if you wish, place salad mixture in individual salad bowls and divide dressing evenly among them. Sprinkle with sunflower seeds. Garnish with radishes.

Makes 4 to 6 servings.

Chafing Dish Spinach Salad

Heated until it just begins to wilt, spinach makes a dramatic first-course salad to prepare at the table — if you are a bit of a culinary exhibitionist.

2 bunches (about ¾ lb *each*) spinach
1 tablespoon olive oil
    Freshly ground black pepper
4 slices bacon, crisply cooked, drained, and crumbled
    Mustard Dressing (recipe follows)
2 hard-cooked eggs, grated
    Lemon wedges

1. Remove and discard stems from spinach; you should have about 15 cups leaves. If done ahead, place in a bowl, cover, and refrigerate.
2. In a deep, broad chafing dish heat olive oil over moderately high heat. Add several grindings of pepper, then bacon. Stir to heat through.
3. Add spinach and mix lightly *just until spinach begins to wilt* (about 1 minute). Remove from heat at once. Mix gently but thoroughly with dressing. Serve salad onto individual plates.
4. Garnish each serving with grated hard-cooked egg and a lemon wedge.

Makes 4 to 6 servings.

Mustard Dressing

In a small bowl mix 2 tablespoons tarragon wine vinegar, 1 tablespoon Dijon mustard, 1 small shallot (finely chopped), ½ teaspoon sugar, an ¼ teaspoon salt. Using a fork or whisk, gradually beat in ⅓ cup salad oil. Makes about ½ cup.

Hot Romaine and Escarole Salad

Here is a second barely wilted salad. It combines two greens with substantial texture—romaine and escarole—in a sweet-sour dressing with bacon and tomato.

2 tablespoons lemon juice
1 tablespoon catsup
1 teaspoon *each* sugar and Dijon mustard
½ teaspoon Worcestershire sauce
1 clove garlic, minced or pressed
6 slices bacon, cut crosswise into ½-inch strips
    Salad oil, if needed
1 medium onion, finely chopped
6 cups torn romaine
4 cups torn escarole
1 medium tomato, cut in thin wedges
    Freshly ground black pepper

1. In a small bowl mix lemon juice, catsup, sugar, mustard, Worcestershire sauce, and garlic.
2. In a large frying pan, electric frying pan, or wok, cook bacon until crisp and brown, stirring often; remove with a slotted spoon and drain. Measure ¼ cup bacon drippings (add oil, if needed, to make ¼ cup or discard any drippings in excess of ¼ cup). In same pan, cook onion in the ¼ cup drippings over medium heat, stirring for about 1 minute. Mix in lemon juice mixture; bring to boiling.
3. To pan add romaine, escarole, and tomato; *immediately* remove from heat. Mix lightly to coat well with dressing. Transfer to a salad bowl and sprinkle with bacon and pepper. Serve at once.

Makes 4 to 6 servings.

Technique Tips —*Cutting Vegetables*

Cucumbers. *Two ways to achieve grooved cucumber slices: (left) cut strips with a lemon-stripping tool, or (right) incise with a table fork. Then slice cucumber thinly.*

Green onions. *Wisps of green onion add character to salads. Cut onion with most of the green stem into long, feathery strips, or cut into 1-inch sections, then into slivers.*

Mushrooms. *Shortly before slicing fresh mushrooms for salad, rinse quickly and pat dry. Slice thinly through stems. Add dressing just before serving to keep mushrooms crisp.*

Cabbage. *A sharp French chef's knife shaves cabbage paper-thin. Cut in half lengthwise; cut out core. Place cut side down, then cut into thin shreds from leafy end.*

❦ Cabbage Salads

Unlike their fragile cousins, leafy green salads, cabbage salads can usually be made well ahead of the time you plan to serve them. Refrigerating them for an hour or more permits flavors to blend and does not make the cabbage less crisp.

You can shred cabbage using a food processor, if you wish. Or you can cut it into delicate shreds with a sharp French chef's knife (page 17). Remove any bruised outer leaves, cut the head in half lengthwise, and remove the core from each half, making a wedge-shaped cut. Place cut sides down and, starting at leafy end, cut each half into the thinnest of shreds.

Creamy Coleslaw

This slaw (the word *cole* comes from the German word for cabbage, *Kohl*) is a favorite accompaniment to hamburgers or delicatessen-style sandwiches.

¾ cup mayonnaise
⅓ cup sour cream
½ teaspoon *each* salt, celery seeds, and prepared mustard
　　Dash pepper
1 teaspoon sugar
1 tablespoon white vinegar
1 small green cabbage (1 to 1¼ lbs), thinly shredded (about 8 cups)
4 green onions, thinly sliced
　　Chopped parsley, for garnish

1. Mix mayonnaise, sour cream, salt, celery seeds, mustard, pepper, sugar, and vinegar thoroughly.
2. Place cabbage and onions in a large bowl. Mix lightly with dressing.
3. Cover and refrigerate for at least 2 hours (up to 8 hours). Sprinkle with parsley.

Makes 6 to 8 servings.

Red-and-Green Cabbage Slaw nestles in outer leaves of a hollowed-out Savoy cabbage. Salad will be most appealing if cabbage is slivered paper-thin; see page 17 for tips on achieving this.

Red-and-Green Cabbage Slaw

Bright with slivers of red and green peppers, this cabbage salad has a zippy oil-and-vinegar dressing.

1 small Savoy (curly) cabbage (about 1½ lbs), thinly shredded
½ cup *each* seeded, slivered red and green bell pepper
½ cup *each* finely chopped fresh parsley and thinly sliced green onions
2 tablespoons sugar
1½ teaspoons salt
½ teaspoon celery seeds
½ cup white vinegar
⅓ cup salad oil

1. In a large bowl mix cabbage, red and green pepper, parsley, and onions.
2. For dressing, shake (in covered jar) or stir together sugar, salt, celery seeds, vinegar, and oil until sugar dissolves.
3. Pour dressing over cabbage mixture; mix lightly. Cover and refrigerate ½ to 3 hours to blend flavors.

Makes 6 to 8 servings.

Red Cabbage Slaw with Dill Dressing

Red-purple cabbage makes one of the handsomest of salads. This one has a sour cream dressing and green onions in abundance.

1 small head (about 2 lbs) red cabbage, thinly shredded
6 green onions, thinly sliced
½ cup sour cream
¼ cup mayonnaise
1 small clove garlic, minced or pressed
1 teaspoon dried dill weed
1 tablespoon *each* lemon juice and white wine vinegar
½ teaspoon salt
¼ teaspoon sugar
⅛ teaspoon white pepper
¼ cup salad oil
Chopped parsley, for garnish

1. In a large bowl combine cabbage and green onions.
2. In a medium bowl mix until smooth sour cream, mayonnaise, garlic, dill weed, lemon juice, vinegar, salt, sugar, and pepper. Using a whisk or fork, gradually beat in oil until well combined.
3. Mix dressing lightly with cabbage mixture. Cover and refrigerate for 1 to 3 hours to blend flavors.
4. Serve sprinkled with parsley.

Makes 6 to 8 servings.

Fruited Cabbage Salad

Adding grapes, mandarin oranges, and pineapple to a ginger-accented coleslaw gives it a more delicate character. This salad is an excellent accompaniment to baked ham.

1 small green cabbage (1 to 1¼ lbs), thinly shredded (about 8 cups)
1 cup halved seedless grapes
1 can (11 oz) mandarin oranges, well drained
1 small can (8 oz) crushed pineapple, well drained
½ cup *each* mayonnaise and sour cream
1 tablespoon finely chopped candied ginger
1 teaspoon grated lemon rind
1 tablespoon lemon juice

1. In a large bowl combine cabbage, grapes, mandarin oranges, and pineapple.
2. In a medium bowl mix mayonnaise, sour cream, ginger, lemon rind, and lemon juice until smooth and well combined.
3. Lightly mix dressing with cabbage mixture. Cover and refrigerate ½ to 3 hours to blend flavors.

Makes 8 servings.

Tangy Blue Cheese Coleslaw

Blue-veined cheese in the dressing complements the assertive flavor of cabbage. You might match this salad with cold roast beef or barbecued steak.

1 medium green cabbage (about 2 lbs), thinly shredded (about 12 cups)
1 small red onion, slivered
¼ cup chopped fresh parsley
1 tablespoon sugar
1 teaspoon salt
¼ cup tarragon wine vinegar
½ cup *each* sour cream and mayonnaise
½ cup crumbled blue-veined cheese

1. In a large bowl lightly mix cabbage, onion, and parsley.
2. In a medium bowl mix sugar and salt; add vinegar and stir until sugar dissolves. Mix in sour cream and mayonnaise until smooth, then fold in cheese.
3. Pour dressing over cabbage mixture. Mix lightly to coat with dressing. Cover and refrigerate for ½ to 3 hours to blend flavors.

Makes 6 to 8 servings.

Chinese Cabbage Toss

A somewhat less familiar member of the cabbage family, Chinese cabbage is also known as Napa or celery cabbage. It is a little less sturdy than other types of cabbage, so this salad should be served soon after it is mixed or it will become soggy.

1 medium Chinese cabbage, shredded (about 8 cups); see note
1 green pepper, quartered, seeded, and cut crosswise into thin strips
½ cup *each* thinly sliced radishes and green onions
2 tablespoons chopped fresh parsley
Sesame Dressing (recipe follows)
¼ cup chopped dry-roasted cashews *or* peanuts

1. In a large bowl combine Chinese cabbage, green pepper, radishes, green onions, and parsley.
2. Mix lightly with Sesame Dressing.
3. Serve sprinkled with cashews or peanuts.

Makes 6 servings.

Note: To prepare cabbage, cut in half lengthwise. Cut out and discard core. To shred, cut crosswise into very thin slices.

Sesame Dressing

Stir 2 tablespoons sesame seeds in a small frying pan over medium heat until lightly browned (6 to 8 minutes); cool slightly. Combine in a covered jar or a bowl sesame seeds, 1 tablespoon sugar, 1 teaspoon salt, 2 teaspoons Oriental sesame oil, ⅓ cup rice wine vinegar, and ¼ cup salad oil. Shake or stir until sugar dissolves. Makes about ⅔ cup.

🌶 *Vegetable Salads*

Vegetables need not be leafy to merit a role in the salad bowl. You can create delightful salads from all kinds of vegetables, raw or cooked. In fact, even leftover vegetables make acceptable salads. If they have been served with butter, rinse with warm water, drain well, blot dry with paper towels, and then add a favorite oil-and-vinegar dressing.

For a change of pace, try some of the following vegetable salads as first courses or accompaniments to the main dish.

Crisp Raw Vegetables with Creamy Curry Dip

Here's a dipping salad you might serve as an hors d'oeuvre. For greatest appeal, cut the vegetables into slender, bite-size strips or slices. No one enjoys a carrot stick as big as a hammer handle. If you prepare the vegetables ahead and refrigerate them in ice water, they will be especially crisp and snappy.

½ cup mayonnaise
½ cup sour cream *or* plain yogurt
1 small clove garlic, minced or pressed
1 tablespoon chili sauce
2 teaspoons curry powder
⅛ teaspoon cayenne pepper
   Raw vegetables for dipping:
      Celery sticks
      Carrot sticks
      Cauliflowerets
      Green and red pepper strips
      Radishes
      Turnip slices
      Cucumber slices

1. For dip, mix mayonnaise, sour cream, garlic, chili sauce, curry powder, and cayenne until smooth. Cover and refrigerate several hours or overnight to blend flavors.
2. Arrange vegetables attractively on a deep platter of crushed ice. Place dip in a bowl or in small individual dishes at each place.

Makes about 1 cup dip; 4 to 6 servings.

Creamy Curry Dip enhances a colorful selection of cold, crisp fresh vegetables.

Green Beans with Mustard Vinaigrette

Ideally this salad would be made with delicate young Blue Lake green beans. But unless you grow this variety yourself, you may not be able to get them. If you use the more common Kentucky Wonder beans, select the smallest you can find.

1 pound small green beans
   Salted water
2 tablespoons tarragon vinegar
1 tablespoon finely chopped shallot *or* red onion
1 tablespoon coarse-grained Dijon mustard
¼ teaspoon salt
1½ tablespoons olive oil
¼ cup salad oil
   Butter lettuce leaves
¼ cup slivered pimiento *or* sweet red bell pepper

1. Snip off ends of beans. Bring a large quantity of salted water to boiling in a large pot. Add beans and boil, uncovered, until tender-crisp (6 to 8 minutes). Pour into a colander to drain. Immediately rinse with cold water to stop cooking. Drain well.
2. In a salad bowl mix vinegar, shallot, mustard, and salt. Using a whisk or fork, gradually beat in oils until dressing is slightly thickened. Add beans and mix lightly.
3. Serve beans on butter lettuce; garnish with pimiento.

Makes 4 to 6 servings.

Homegrown sprouts are packed with more flavor than the commercially grown kind, and they are fun to watch develop in just 3 to 4 days in your kitchen. Clockwise from left alfalfa sprouts (in dish), mung bean sprouts, radish sprouts, and azuki bean sprouts.

Grow Your Own Sprouts

Sprouts, the edible shoots of seeds, are easy to grow in your own kitchen. By growing your own, you can have greater variety than the usual bean and alfalfa sprouts available in supermarkets. But even these standbys are fun to raise at home.

Most sprouts can be transformed from seed or bean to a crop that can be harvested and enjoyed, in about 4 days. They are great in all kinds of salads and sandwiches in place of lettuce —keep this in mind when other greens are scarce or expensive. Flavors are distinctive, as you will discover if you try several kinds.

You can sprout practically any seed, but some of the favorites are alfalfa seeds; mung and azuki beans; soy beans; lentils; dried peas; wheat berries; raw hulled sunflower seeds; curled cress; and dill, radish, and mustard seeds.

The easiest container to use for any of these is a 1-quart jar. Alfalfa sprouts, or any other seeds as small, can also be sprouted in a shallow dish.

Seeds and legumes you can't find in a grocery store are sold in garden stores and in health food stores. You can also buy sprouting equipment and packaged seeds by mail from:

Sprouts are Good
226 Hamilton Avenue
Palo Alto, California 94301

The simple steps in sprouting are:

1. Soak seeds overnight in water to cover; rinse and drain 3 times; then drain well.
2. Place seeds in a 1-quart glass jar such as a canning jar. Cover opening with cheesecloth or a stainless steel screen secured by the jar ring. Place jar *on its side* in a warm, dark place (such as a cupboard next to or above the refrigerator) or on the kitchen counter, covered with a kitchen towel (leave opening uncovered for ventilation).
3. Let stand until sprouts reach a length of 1 to 1½ inches (in the case of alfalfa and other small sprouts, until they have 2 leaves), from 2 to 4 days. During this time, rinse well and drain twice a day—once in the morning and again in the evening. When you rinse the sprouting seeds, fill the jar with enough lukewarm water to submerge the sprouts; they should have room to swirl about. Then drain, shaking gently to remove most of the water.
4. When the sprouts are big enough, leave the jar on the counter in indirect light for several hours. This will turn the leaves green.
5. Finally, rinse the sprouts, drain well, and pat dry. Refrigerate them in the jar or a plastic bag until you are ready to use them. They will stay fresh in the refrigerator for up to a week.

For a 1-quart jar, use the following amount of seeds:

Mung, azuki, or soy beans—¼ cup

Lentils—¼ cup

Dried peas—¼ cup

Wheat berries—¼ cup

Raw, hulled sunflower seeds—¼ cup

Radish seeds—2 tablespoons

Alfalfa, mustard, dill, or curly cress seeds—1½ teaspoons

For any of the small seeds, an alternative method—and one that is fun to watch—is to grow the sprouts in a small dish.

Fold several layers of cheesecloth or cotton batting to fit the dish. Place in dish and slowly pour in lukewarm water until saturated. Sprinkle on presoaked seeds in a single layer. Let stand at room temperature, moistening cloth occasionally if it becomes dry.

Seeds should burst in 24 to 36 hours and the shoots appear. They are ready to use in 2 to 4 days, as soon as most of the sprouts have 2 leaves. Brush off clinging seed cases; then pluck sprouts or cut them with kitchen scissors.

An oil-and-vinegar dressing with garlic and lemon turns lightly cooked broccoli into a dazzling salad. For best color, wait to add dressing until ready to serve.

Lemony Marinated Broccoli Salad

Lemon and garlic accent tender-crisp broccoli, garnished with threads of lemon rind and toasted walnuts.

1 bunch (1¼ to 1½ lbs) broccoli
  Salted water
  Lemon-Garlic Vinaigrette Dressing (recipe follows)
  Slivered lemon rind and coarsely chopped toasted walnuts, for garnish

1. Cut off broccoli flowerets and separate into bite-size pieces. Trim and discard ends of stems and peel lower portion of stems. Slice stems crosswise ¼ inch thick.
2. Cook flowers and stems in a small amount of boiling salted water (or steam on a rack) until tender-crisp (4 to 6 minutes). Place in a colander; then rinse well with cold water to cool broccoli. Drain well. If done ahead, refrigerate until ready to assemble salad.
3. Mix broccoli lightly with dressing. Arrange in a serving dish and garnish with lemon rind and walnuts.

Makes 4 to 6 servings.

Lemon-Garlic Vinaigrette Dressing

In a small bowl mix 1½ tablespoons lemon juice, 1 tablespoon white wine vinegar, 1 clove garlic (minced or pressed), 1 teaspoon grated lemon rind, ¼ teaspon *each* salt and dried oregano, and ⅛ teaspoon seasoned pepper. Using a fork or whisk, gradually beat in 2 tablespoons olive oil and ¼ cup salad oil until smooth and well blended. Makes about ⅓ cup.

Marinated Bean Salad

Italian (or Romano) green beans, combined with canned red kidney and garbanzo beans, make a vivid looking — and tasting — picnic salad.

1 pound Italian green beans
  Salted water
1 can (15 oz) red kidney beans, drained
1 small can (8¾ oz) garbanzo beans (ceci beans or chick peas), drained
1 sweet red (or green) bell pepper, seeded and slivered
½ cup *each* slivered mild red onion and chopped celery
2 tablespoons sweet pickle relish
  Mustard-Herb Vinaigrette Dressing (recipe follows)

1. Snip off ends of beans; cut into 1½-inch lengths. Bring a large quantity of salted water to boiling in a large pot. Add green beans and boil, uncovered, until beans are tender-crisp (4 to 6 minutes). Pour into a colander to drain. Immediately rinse with cold water to stop cooking. Drain well.
2. Mix green beans, kidney beans, garbanzo beans, red or green pepper, onion, and celery. Stir pickle relish into dressing. Combine dressing gently with bean mixture.
3. Cover and refrigerate for 3 hours or longer (up to 8 hours) to blend flavors.

Makes 6 to 8 servings.

Mustard-Herb Vinaigrette Dressing

In a small bowl mix 2 tablespoons cider vinegar, 1 clove garlic (minced or pressed), 1 tablespoon Dijon mustard, 2 tablespoons chopped fresh parsley, ¼ teaspoon *each* salt and sugar, ⅛ teaspoon *each* dried thyme and oregano, and a dash of seasoned pepper. Using a whisk or fork, gradually beat in 2 tablespoons olive oil and ¼ cup salad oil. Makes about ½ cup.

Curried Vegetable Salad

Here is a salad that is both colorful and boldly flavored. If sweet red bell pepper isn't available, substitute a green one and add a small jar of chopped pimiento for color. This salad is a good companion for roast turkey or lamb.

1 medium cauliflower
   (1 to 1¼ lbs)
   Salted water
1 jar (6 oz) marinated artichoke hearts, drained
1 sweet red bell pepper, quartered, seeded, and slivered
1 medium zucchini, quartered lengthwise and sliced ¼ inch thick
3 green onions, thinly sliced
   Curry Dressing (recipe follows)
   Romaine leaves

1. Remove and discard cauliflower leaves. Cut out core and break cauliflower into bite-size flowerets.
2. Cook flowerets in a small amount of boiling salted water (or steam on a rack) just until tender-crisp (5 to 7 minutes). Place in a colander; then rinse with cold water to cool cauliflower. Drain well.
3. Combine cauliflower, artichokes, red pepper, zucchini, and green onions. Mix lightly with Curry Dressing. Cover and refrigerate at least 3 hours to blend flavors.
4. Serve in a romaine-lined bowl.

Makes 4 to 6 servings.

Curry Dressing

In a medium bowl combine 2 tablespoons white wine vinegar, 1 tablespoon lemon juice, 1½ teaspoons curry powder, ½ teaspoon mustard seeds (slightly crushed), ¼ teaspoon *each* salt and grated lemon rind, and 1 clove garlic (minced or pressed). Using a whisk or fork, gradually beat in ⅓ cup olive oil or salad oil until well blended. Makes about ½ cup.

This curried salad includes cauliflower, artichokes, pepper, and zucchini.

Marinated Cauliflower Salad

This cauliflower salad can be made well ahead of serving time, to enable the pungent flavor of the dressing to be absorbed by the vegetable. Radishes and parsley, added at the end, provide vivid accents.

1 medium cauliflower
   (1 to 1¼ lbs)
   Salted water
¼ cup tarragon wine vinegar
1 teaspoon Dijon mustard
¼ teaspoon salt
   Dash white pepper
3 tablespoons salad oil
½ cup thinly sliced radishes
   Chopped parsley, for garnish

1. Remove and discard cauliflower leaves. Cut out core and break cauliflower into bite-size flowerets.
2. Cook flowerets in a small amount of boiling salted water (or steam on a rack) just until tender-crisp (5 to 7 minutes). Place in a colander; then rinse with cold water to cool cauliflower. Drain well.
3. In a small bowl combine vinegar, mustard, salt, and pepper. Using a fork or whisk, gradually beat in oil until well combined. Pour over cauliflower in a shallow bowl. Cover and refrigerate 6 to 8 hours or overnight.
4. Just before serving, add radishes, mixing to combine with marinade. Sprinkle with parsley.

Makes 4 to 6 servings.

Sweet-Sour Marinated Summer Squash

If you grow golden zucchini in your garden, this salad is a fine showplace for the vegetable. Small crookneck squash can also be used.

3 medium green zucchini (about ¾ lb), thinly sliced
3 small crookneck squash *or* yellow zucchini (about ½ lb), thinly sliced
3 green onions, thinly sliced
½ cup finely chopped sweet red bell pepper
¼ cup sugar
1 teaspoon salt
¼ teaspoon seasoned pepper
¼ cup red wine vinegar
⅔ cup cider vinegar
⅓ cup salad oil
   Lettuce leaves
   Chopped parsley, for garnish

1. In a large bowl mix zucchini, crookneck squash, green onions, and red pepper.
2. In a medium bowl mix sugar, salt, pepper, and vinegars, stirring until sugar dissolves. Using a fork or whisk, gradually beat in oil.
3. Mix dressing lightly with zucchini mixture. Cover and refrigerate for 4 to 6 hours or overnight to blend flavors.
4. Serve in a bowl lined with lettuce. Sprinkle with parsley.

Makes 6 servings.

Leeks Vinaigrette

Pungent leeks in an assertive oil-and-vinegar dressing are a favorite beginning for a French dinner. Accompany with a crusty *baguette*. You can serve this salad warm or at room temperature.

1 bunch (4 or 5) leeks
  Salted water
  Mustard-Herb Vinaigrette Dressing (recipe follows)
1 hard-cooked egg, sliced
  Tomato wedges and ripe olives, for garnish

1. Cut off root ends of leeks; remove coarse outer leaves. Cut off green tops so leeks are about 9 inches long. Split lengthwise, from stem end, cutting to within about 1 inch of root ends. Soak in cold water for several minutes; then separate leaves under running water to rinse away any clinging grit; drain.

2. Place leeks side by side in a broad frying pan in about 1 inch of boiling salted water; cover and simmer until tender (8 to 10 minutes). With a slotted spoon, remove carefully to 2 individual au gratin dishes.
3. Pour dressing evenly over leeks. Garnish with egg slices, tomato wedges, and olives.

Makes 2 servings.

Mustard-Herb Vinaigrette Dressing

In a small bowl mix 1 tablespoon *each* tarragon wine vinegar and lemon juice, ⅛ teaspoon *each* salt and dried thyme, 1 teaspoon Dijon mustard, and a dash white pepper. Using a whisk or fork, gradually beat in 2 tablespoons olive oil and ¼ cup salad oil until smooth and well combined. Just before using, mix in 1 tablespoon chopped fresh parsley. Makes about ½ cup.

Technique Tips — *Cutting Vegetables*

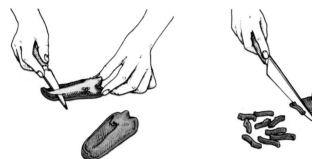

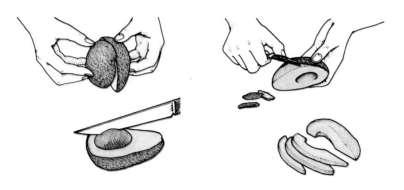

Peppers. To make red or green bell pepper strips, first cut pepper lengthwise into quarters, cutting out and discarding the core and any seeds (left). Then slice each quarter crosswise into thin strips as shown at right.

Avocados. To peel and pit, first cut ripe avocado lengthwise around center, cutting all the way to seed. Separate by turning each half in opposite direction. Impale seed on knife and turn to remove it. Then peel and slice with a knife.

❧ Tomato Salads

Technically, tomatoes are a fruit, not a vegetable. But most of us probably serve them as vegetables, and certainly they are a popular element in salads.

When tomatoes are tender and ripe, it is not necessary to peel them. There are times, however, when it is aesthetically more pleasing to serve them peeled. The easiest way to peel a tomato is to dip it for a few seconds into boiling water. The skin then becomes almost papery and can be slipped off easily.

Sliced Tomatoes with Pesto Dressing

Pesto is a fragrant green sauce that many people regard as one of Genoa's greatest gifts to the world. Made with fresh basil, olive oil, and Parmesan cheese, it is a natural complement to tomatoes.

2 tablespoons red wine vinegar
¼ cup lightly packed fresh basil leaves (or 1 tablespoon dried basil and 3 tablespoons chopped fresh parsley)
1 clove garlic, minced or pressed
¼ teaspoon *each* salt and sugar
¼ cup grated Parmesan cheese
⅓ cup olive oil or salad oil
3 large or 5 to 6 medium tomatoes
  Lettuce leaves
  Freshly ground black pepper
  Toasted pine nuts (optional)

1. In blender or food processor combine vinegar, basil, garlic, salt, sugar, Parmesan cheese, and olive oil. Whirl or process until smooth and well combined. Let stand at room temperature for 1 to 2 hours to blend flavors. Stir well with a whisk or fork before using.
2. Core tomatoes (peel first, if you wish). Slice about ½ inch thick. Arrange in a shallow lettuce-lined serving bowl or on lettuce on individual plates. Grind pepper over tomatoes to taste.
3. Drizzle tomatoes evenly with *pesto*. Garnish with pine nuts, if you wish.

Makes 4 to 6 servings.

Fresh basil makes an irresistible dressing for perfectly ripe summer tomatoes. Toasted pine nuts are an optional accent.

Taste-of-Gazpacho Salad

This attractively arranged tomato salad has all the elements of that popular cold Spanish soup, *gazpacho*. It makes a fine summer lunch with French rolls, goat cheese, and a red jug wine. It can also be served as a first course.

  Red leaf lettuce
3 medium tomatoes, sliced
½ medium cucumber, scored (see page 17) and thinly sliced
1 avocado, halved, peeled, seeded, and diced
¼ cup *each* chopped mild red onion and green pepper
  Olive Oil and Garlic Dressing (recipe follows)
½ cup Garlic Croutons (see page 26)

1. Line a platter or serving plate with lettuce. Arrange tomatoes in rows in center. Arrange cucumber at one side, and avocado cubes at other side of tomatoes.
2. Sprinkle onion over cucumber and avocado; sprinkle green pepper over tomatoes. Drizzle about a third of the dressing over salad.
3. Sprinkle salad with croutons. Serve remaining dressing in a small bowl or pitcher to add at table.

Makes 6 servings.

Olive Oil and Garlic Dressing

In a medium bowl mix 3 tablespoons red wine vinegar, ½ teaspoon *each* salt and dried oregano, 1 clove garlic (minced or pressed), and ⅛ teaspoon cayenne pepper. Using a whisk or fork, gradually beat in ½ cup olive oil (or ¼ cup *each* olive oil and salad oil) until well combined. Makes about ¾ cup.

Tomato and Red Pepper Salad

Scarlet tomatoes and pepper strips make a delicious salad with a fresh basil dressing.

  Basil Dressing (recipe follows)
3 large or 6 medium tomatoes
1 red bell pepper, quartered, seeded, and cut into thin strips
  Escarole or leaf lettuce
  Freshly ground black pepper

1. Prepare dressing and let it stand for at least 1 hour to blend flavors.
2. Peel and slice tomatoes. Arrange tomatoes and pepper strips in a shallow bowl lined with escarole or lettuce. Drizzle evenly with dressing. Grind pepper over salad to taste.

Makes 4 to 6 servings.

Basil Dressing

In blender combine 2 tablespoons *each* salad oil and olive oil, 2 tablespoons red wine vinegar, 1 clove garlic (minced or pressed), ½ teaspoon *each* salt and sugar, and ⅓ cup lightly packed fresh basil leaves. Whirl until well blended. Makes about ⅓ cup.

Tomatoes Stuffed with Cottage Cheese and Peas

Here is a pretty tomato salad to serve as a first course, or for a light lunch with wheat or rye crackers and iced tea.

2 cups small curd cottage cheese
½ teaspoon *each* dried dill weed and dry mustard
⅛ teaspoon seasoned pepper
4 green onions, thinly sliced
1 cup thawed frozen peas
¼ pound small peeled, cooked shrimp
6 medium tomatoes
  Salt
  Watercress sprigs, for garnish

1. Mix cottage cheese, dill weed, mustard, and seasoned pepper until well combined. Fold in green onions, peas, and shrimp. If prepared ahead, cover and refrigerate.
2. To serve, core tomatoes (peel first, if you wish). Separate each into 6 wedges, cutting almost to, *but not through,* bottom. Spread sections slightly. Salt cut surfaces lightly.
3. Divide cottage cheese mixture evenly among the 6 tomatoes, filling them attractively. Garnish with watercress.

Makes 6 servings.

Hearts of Palm Salad

Garlic Lamb Chops

Baked Potatoes   Green Beans

Minted Chocolate Mousse

Zinfandel   Coffee

🐾 Dinner for Two

A salad with several taste-tingling elements makes an enticing first course for a special dinner.

Make-ahead elements of this simple but festive dinner include the salad mixture—hearts of palm and tiny shrimp, marinated in a tarragon-and-lime dressing — and the dessert mousse.

Put the potatoes in to bake before you assemble the salad. Green beans cook while you prepare the lamb chops.

The salad serves 4; to prepare it for 2, use half the romaine and tomato and just 1 hard-cooked egg. You might as well make the full amount of dressing, hearts of palm, and shrimp. Any of the mixture you don't use for the salad will make a fine supper for one the next day.

Hearts of Palm Salad

1 tablespoon *each* tarragon vinegar and lime or lemon juice
2 teaspoons Dijon mustard
1 clove garlic, minced or pressed
¾ teaspoon salt
½ teaspoon sugar
¼ teaspoon dried tarragon
   Dash cayenne pepper
2 tablespoons olive oil
¼ cup salad oil
1 can (14 oz) hearts of palm, drained and sliced in ¼-inch-thick rounds
6 ounces small peeled, cooked shrimp (see page 75)

1 head romaine
1 medium tomato, cut in wedges
2 hard-cooked eggs, sliced

1. In a medium bowl mix vinegar, lime juice, mustard, garlic, salt, sugar, tarragon, and cayenne. Using a whisk or fork, gradually beat in olive oil and salad oil until slightly thickened and well blended. Lightly mix in hearts of palm and shrimp. Cover and refrigerate for 1 to 2 hours to blend flavors.
2. Line salad bowl or individual salad plates with outer leaves of romaine. Shred inner leaves and use to top whole leaves.
3. Serve hearts of palm mixture on romaine. Garnish with tomato wedges and egg slices.

Makes 4 servings.

Note: This salad also makes a fine main dish for lunch. If you serve it as a main course, increase the shrimp to ½ pound to make 3 servings.

Homemade Croutons, Easy and Good

Making your own salad croutons is simple—all it takes are a few slices of day-old (or older) bread. Homemade croutons are much fresher and more flavorful than the packaged kind. Once you have tasted any of the following, you will never again spend money on store-bought croutons.

Any croutons that aren't used within a day or two should be stored in a cool place in an opaque, airtight container. They can also be frozen.

Garlic Croutons

Cut crusts from 5 slices firm white bread or 6 slices French bread. Dice bread into ½-inch cubes. In a large frying pan over medium heat, heat 2 tablespoons *each* butter or margarine and olive oil or salad oil. Mix in 1 clove garlic (minced or pressed). Add bread cubes, stirring until well coated with butter mixture. Transfer bread cubes to a rimmed baking sheet and spread in a single layer. Bake in a 300°F oven until lightly browned and crisp (25 to 30 minutes). Cool. Makes about 2 cups.

Parmesan Croutons

Prepare as for Garlic Croutons. To butter mixture add ¼ teaspoon paprika. With bread cubes, stir in ¼ cup grated Parmesan cheese.

Herbed Croutons

Prepare as for Garlic Croutons. To butter mixture add ¼ teaspoon *each* dried oregano, thyme, crumbled rosemary, and basil.

Sesame Croutons

Prepare as for Garlic Croutons, omitting garlic. Substitute 1 tablespoon Oriental sesame oil for 1 tablespoon of the olive oil or salad oil. With bread cubes, stir in 1 tablespoon sesame seeds.

Bacon-Onion Croutons

Prepare as for Garlic Croutons, omitting garlic. Substitute 2 tablespoons bacon drippings for butter or margarine. To oil mixture add ½ teaspoon onion powder and 1 teaspoon poppy seeds.

Dilled Rye Croutons

Substitute 6 slices oval or round rye bread for white or French bread. To butter mixture add 1 teaspoon dried dill weed.

Garlic Lamb Chops

1 tablespoon butter or margarine

2 teaspoons peanut oil or salad oil

6 whole cloves garlic

6 small rib lamb chops (about 1½ lbs), about ¾ inch thick
  White pepper

⅛ teaspoon *each* dried thyme and crumbled rosemary
  Salt

1 shallot, finely chopped

½ cup dry white wine

½ teaspoon Dijon mustard

¼ teaspoon paprika
  Watercress, for garnish

1. Heat butter and oil in a 10-inch frying pan. Add garlic and cook, stirring occasionally, over medium heat until garlic is golden-brown; remove and reserve garlic.

2. Meanwhile, sprinkle lamb chops evenly on both sides with pepper, thyme, and rosemary. In same pan in which garlic was cooked, brown lamb chops well on both sides over medium-high heat, cooking 3 to 5 minutes per side for pink centers. Remove lamb chops to a warm serving dish and keep warm; salt to taste.

3. Pour off most of the fat in pan. Add shallot and stir until it begins to brown. Mix in reserved garlic, wine, mustard, and paprika. Boil, stirring to incorporate pan drippings, until liquid is reduced by about half.

4. Pour sauce over lamb chops. Garnish with watercress.

Makes 2 servings.

Minted Chocolate Mousse

1 square (1 oz) semisweet chocolate

½ square (½ oz) unsweetened chocolate

2 teaspoons light corn syrup

1½ tablespoons white crème de menthe

2 eggs, separated
  Dash cream of tartar

1 tablespoon sugar

⅓ cup whipping cream
  Candied violets and fresh mint, for garnish

1. Melt chocolate over hot but not boiling water. Stir in corn syrup and crème de menthe until smoothly blended. Remove from heat.

2. Beat egg whites with cream of tartar until soft peaks form. Add sugar gradually, beating until stiff. Using the same beaters, beat egg yolks until thick and pale; blend into chocolate mixture. Fold in egg whites.

3. Whip cream until stiff; fold into chocolate mixture. Pour the mousse into 2 individual serving dishes. Refrigerate for 2 to 3 hours or overnight.

4. Serve garnished with dollops of whipped cream, candied violets, and mint.

Makes 2 servings.

Salad featuring hearts of palm sets the pace for a candlelit dinner for two with lamb chops and chocolate mousse.

Molded Salads

The closest thing to controversy in the salad world may be over gelatin salads. Salads of this sort seem to have as many opponents as enthusiasts. Those in the first group tend to shudder at the thought of carrots in lemon gelatin or celery in a tomato aspic, murmuring phrases such as "quivering death"!

Gelatin salads fans, undeterred, keep bouncing back. One finds their work on buffet tables the world over. And no one can deny the handsomeness or convenience of their results.

One of the enticements of molded salads is the fact that they are made well in advance of serving. They shimmer with jewel-like colors and can hold a wealth of good-tasting foods. They are served as first courses, accompaniments, main dishes, or desserts. With thought and care, your gelatin salads can delight even the staunchest opponents of this genre.

The essential ingredient of a molded salad is gelatin, either flavored or unflavored. Packaged, flavored gelatins offer sparkling jellybean colors and distinct — though, for many, overly sweet — flavors. Unflavored gelatin gives more creative freedom: One can add liquids such as fruit or vegetable juice, broth, or wine to arrive at more natural flavors.

Salad molds in fanciful variety offer inspiration to those who enjoy creating gelatin salads. You can embellish these salads with fruits, vegetables, meats, or seafoods. The recipe for the rabbit-shaped Carrot and Pineapple Salad appears on page 31.

In creating your own combinations, remember one simple rule of thumb: A standard 3-ounce package of flavored gelatin or an envelope of unflavored gelatin will thicken about 2 cups of liquid, in which can be suspended about 1½ cups of solids such as chopped fruit, vegetables, meat, or seafood. Too much gelatin can make the texture of your salad tough or rubbery.

Unflavored gelatin is usually first soaked in a little liquid for several minutes, during which time you can see the granules soften and expand. Then the mixture is heated to dissolve the gelatin completely. When you do this, be sure no particles cling to the sides or bottom of the pan—stir until the mixture is clear. Flavored gelatin is simply dissolved in boiling liquid.

You can add fruits or other foods after the gelatin mixture has chilled long enough to thicken slightly and become syrupy. It should have the consistency of unbeaten egg whites. Solids added to the mixture any sooner will sink to the bottom, rather than remaining dispersed.

There are few limits to the foods that can be added to a gelatin-based salad. One, however, is fresh or frozen pineapple. It contains an enzyme that prevents a gel from forming. Canned pineapple or pineapple juice does not present this problem.

Usually a gelatin salad will be ready to unmold after 3 to 4 hours in the refrigerator, although the size of the salad, the temperature of added ingredients, and the size and shape of the mold all affect chilling time.

Although gelatin salads are usually made well ahead of serving, it is not wise to expect them to be in top form longer than 24 hours. After that the gelatin is very likely to become rubbery.

For many, the act of getting a gelatin salad out of its mold is the moment of truth in its creation. The best method is to dip the mold *quickly* into a pan of very hot water; this should take no more than 5 seconds. If you see a slight movement of the salad within the mold, or a little melting at the edges as you try to slide the salad from side to side, you will know it is ready to be removed. Too long in the hot water will melt some of the gelatin, destroying detail and shape.

Place the serving plate over the mold, invert it rapidly, and give the salad a firm shake or tap. It should drop smoothly onto the plate. Sometimes it may be necessary to slip a thin-bladed knife between the salad and the mold to release the vacuum holding the gelatin in place. Then, if it doesn't come right out, leave the mold inverted on the plate for a few minutes and let gravity do its work.

For a creamy gelatin salad you can oil the mold or spray it with a nonstick coating. These substances are not especially compatible with clear gelatins, however.

After you remove the salad from the mold, return it to the refrigerator for ½ hour or longer before you serve it. Of course, it is not essential to make a gelatin salad in a fancy mold. It will taste much the same if prepared in a square or rectangular pan, although the most dedicated salad-molders are convinced this takes some of the sport out of the process.

Molded Asparagus Mousse

Fresh asparagus makes these creamy individual salads a spring indulgence. Serve them with a dressing of chopped watercress in a whipped cream-and-mayonnaise mixture. This salad works well as a first course.

1 envelope unflavored gelatin
¾ cup water
3 cups cut asparagus
¼ teaspoon dried tarragon
½ cup whipping cream
¼ teaspoon grated lemon peel
1 tablespoon lemon juice
¼ cup dry vermouth
½ teaspoon salt
⅛ teaspoon white paper
   Watercress Cream Dressing (recipe follows)
   Cherry tomatoes and watercress sprigs, for garnish

1. Sprinkle gelatin over water in a small saucepan; let stand 5 minutes. Place over medium heat, stirring until gelatin dissolves; set aside.

2. Steam asparagus on a rack over boiling water until just tender (6 to 8 minutes); remove and set aside 12 tips.

3. Place remaining asparagus in blender or food processor with tarragon and cream; whirl or process until smoothly puréed. Mix in lemon peel, lemon juice, vermouth, salt, pepper, and gelatin mixture. Refrigerate, stirring occasionally, until mixture begins to set.

4. Arrange 3 asparagus tips in bottom of each of four 1-cup molds. Divide asparagus mixture evenly into the 4 molds. Cover and chill until firm (at least 3 hours).

5. To serve, unmold and place each mousse on a chilled plate, top with a dollop of dressing, and garnish with tomatoes and watercress. Serve additional dressing in a bowl, to add to each salad to taste.

Makes 4 servings.

Watercress Cream Dressing

Whip ⅓ cup cream with ⅛ teaspoon *each* salt and dry mustard and a dash white pepper until stiff. Fold into ½ cup mayonnaise, to which ¼ cup chopped watercress leaves have been added. Makes about 1¼ cups.

Spinach Molded Salad with Shrimp Sauce

You might serve this creamy green salad on fresh spinach leaves.

1 package (3 oz) lime-flavored gelatin
1 cup boiling water
2 tablespoons sherry wine vinegar
½ cup mayonnaise
1 cup small curd cottage cheese
3 green onions, thinly sliced
1 stalk celery, thinly sliced
1 cup lightly packed slivered spinach leaves
   Spinach leaves, whole, for garnish
   Shrimp Sauce (recipe follows)

1. In a large bowl mix gelatin and boiling water, stirring until gelatin dissolves. Stir in vinegar, then mayonnaise, mixing until well combined.

2. In blender or food processor, whirl or process cottage cheese until smooth and creamy. Stir into gelatin mixture. Refrigerate until set; then beat until mixture is frothy.

3. Fold in onions, celery, and spinach. Pour into a 4-cup mold. Refrigerate until firm (3 to 4 hours).

4. Unmold onto a serving plate. Garnish with spinach leaves. Accompany with Shrimp Sauce.

Makes 6 servings.

Shrimp Sauce

Mix ½ cup *each* mayonnaise and sour cream, ¼ cup chili sauce, 1 tablespoon *each* lemon juice and prepared horseradish, and ½ teaspoon Worcestershire sauce until smooth. Mix in 1 stalk celery (finely chopped), 2 tablespoons chopped fresh parsley, and ¼ pound small peeled, cooked shrimp. Makes about 2 cups.

Avocado Loaf with Filbert Dressing

Strips of avocado are revealed in an enticing mosaic at the center of this molded salad loaf as slices are cut. Of French origin, it is accompanied by a toasted filbert dressing.

2   envelopes unflavored gelatin
1   cup water
3   large ripe avocados
3   tablespoons lime juice
¼   cup dry sherry
1   cup sour cream
1   tablespoon Dijon mustard
½   teaspoon salt
⅛   teaspoon white pepper
    Watercress sprigs
    Filbert Dressing (recipe follows)

1. Sprinkle gelatin over water in a small saucepan; let stand 5 minutes. Place over medium heat, stirring until gelatin dissolves; set aside.

2. Peel and pit 2 of the avocados; place in food processor or blender with lime juice and sherry. Process or whirl until smoothly puréed. Mix in sour cream, mustard, salt, pepper, and gelatin mixture.

Even those who are not usually enthralled by gelatin salads may change their tune at the first taste of the creamy fresh asparagus salad at left. Made in individual fluted molds, the salad is served as a first course with a frothy whipped cream and watercress dressing.

3. Cover and refrigerate, stirring occasionally, until mixture begins to set. Peel and pit remaining avocado; slice lengthwise.

4. Pour half of the gelatin mixture into an oiled 4½- by 8½-inch loaf pan. Top with avocado slices in parallel rows; then cover with remaining gelatin mixture. Cover and chill until firm (at least 3 hours).

5. To serve, unmold loaf and cut into slices. Serve on chilled salad plates, garnished with sprigs of watercress. Spoon a little Filbert Dressing over each serving.

Makes 8 servings.

Filbert Dressing

Spread ¼ cup coarsely chopped filberts (or almonds) in a shallow pan. Bake in a 350°F oven until lightly browned (8 to 10 minutes). Cool slightly. In a small bowl, mix 2 tablespoons tarragon wine vinegar, 2 teaspoons Dijon mustard, 1 shallot (finely chopped), ⅛ teaspoon salt, and a dash of white pepper. Using a whisk or fork, gradually beat in 2 tablespoons filbert oil or olive oil and ¼ cup salad oil. Mix in filberts. Makes about ⅔ cup.

Carrot and Pineapple Salad

Tangy citrus flavors enhance this favorite salad combination.

1   small can (8 oz) crushed pineapple
    Cold water
1   envelope unflavored gelatin
¼   cup sugar
¼   teaspoon salt
3   tablespoons lemon juice
1   teaspoon grated lemon rind
1   cup water
½   cup finely shredded carrots
    Lettuce leaves or alfalfa sprouts
    Sour cream *or* plain yogurt

1. Drain pineapple, reserving liquid. Measure liquid; add cold water, if needed, to make ½ cup. Place liquid in a small pan and sprinkle gelatin over it. Let stand 5 minutes. Place over low heat and stir until gelatin dissolves.

2. Remove from heat and mix in sugar, salt, lemon juice, lemon rind, and the 1 cup water, stirring until

sugar dissolves. Pour into a medium bowl. Refrigerate, stirring occasionally, until mixture begins to thicken and becomes syrupy. Fold in pineapple and carrots.

3. Pour into a 2½- to 3-cup mold; refrigerate until firm (2 to 3 hours).

4. Unmold onto a serving plate. Serve on individual plates lined with lettuce or alfalfa sprouts; add a dollop of sour cream or yogurt.

Makes 4 servings.

Sweet-Sour Beet Salad

Here is a tart-sweet crimson salad that makes a bright addition to a holiday dinner table with roast turkey or chicken. If you make it in a ring mold, serve the creamy dressing in a small bowl in the center.

1   large package (6 oz) raspberry-flavored gelatin
1½ cups boiling water
½   cup sweet pickle juice
1   can (1 lb) julienne beets
1   small can (8 oz) crushed pineapple, well drained (reserve liquid)
    Chicory, for garnish
    Tangy Dressing (recipe follows)

1. In a large bowl mix gelatin and boiling water, stirring until gelatin dissolves. Stir in pickle juice. Drain beets, reserving liquid; add water to beet liquid to make 2 cups. Mix into gelatin mixture. Refrigerate, stirring occasionally, until mixture is slightly thickened and syrupy.

2. Fold in beets and pineapple. Pour into a 6-cup mold. Refrigerate until firm (about 4 hours).

3. Unmold onto a serving plate. Garnish with chicory. Pass dressing to add to individual servings at the table.

Makes 6 to 8 servings.

Tangy Dressing

In a medium bowl mix until smooth ½ cup sour cream, ¼ cup mayonnaise, and 2 tablespoons of the liquid drained from pineapple. Mix in 1 tablespoon chili sauce, 1 teaspoon Dijon mustard, 2 green onions (thinly sliced), and 2 tablespoons finely chopped sweet pickles. Makes about 1 cup.

Layered Cherry-Pineapple Salad

This salad requires a little more work than others, for it is really two salads in one. The top half is a creamy coconut-pineapple salad, in contrast to a bottom layer of tart, spiced cherries in clear crimson gelatin.

1   cup boiling water
1   package (3 oz) lemon-flavored gelatin
1   small can (8 oz) crushed pineapple
1   cup cottage cheese
½   teaspoon vanilla
¼   cup flaked coconut
1   can (l lb) pitted red tart cherries
1   package (3 oz) cherry-flavored gelatin
¼   teaspoon ground cinnamon
½   cup chopped toasted walnuts

1. In a mixing bowl pour boiling water over lemon gelatin, stirring until gelatin dissolves. Drain pineapple, reserving liquid. Place pineapple liquid in blender or food processor with cottage cheese and vanilla. Whirl or process until smooth and creamy. Add cottage cheese to gelatin mixture, stirring until well combined. Refrigerate until mixture is slightly thickened.
2. Fold in drained pineapple and coconut. Place in a 6-cup mold and refrigerate until almost set.
3. Drain cherries, reserving liquid. Add water to make 2 cups. Heat liquid to boiling. Pour over cherry gelatin and cinnamon in a mixing bowl. Stir until gelatin dissolves. Refrigerate until mixture is slightly thickened and syrupy.
4. Mix in drained cherries and walnuts. Spread over pineapple layer in mold. Refrigerate until firm (3 to 4 hours).
5. Unmold onto a serving plate.

Makes 8 servings.

Rosé wine is the medium in which such fresh summer fruits as raspberries, strawberries, and cherries are suspended. The salad is so subtle and delicate it can be served as a light dessert. Slightly soured cream makes the dressing.

Berries and Cherries Rosé

Rosé wine is the piquant medium for this delicate summer salad with raspberries, strawberries, and sweet cherries. Although it is not overly sweet, you might serve this for a light dessert on a sultry day.

1   envelope unflavored gelatin
2   tablespoons sugar
¾   cup boiling water
1¼ cups rosé wine
½   cup *each* raspberries and halved strawberries
1   cup pitted sweet cherries
    Whipped Crème Fraîche (recipe follows)

1. In a medium bowl mix gelatin and sugar. Add boiling water and stir until gelatin dissolves completely; stir in wine.
2. Refrigerate, stirring occasionally, until mixture begins to thicken and becomes syrupy. Fold in berries and cherries.
3. Pour into a 4-cup mold or six ¾-cup individual molds; refrigerate until firm (3 to 4 hours).
4. Unmold onto one or more serving plates. Serve with Whipped Crème Fraîche.

Makes 6 servings.

Whipped Crème Fraîche

Heat ½ cup whipping cream until barely warm to the touch (90° to 100°F). Stir in 1 tablespoon buttermilk or sour cream. Let stand at room temperature (68° to 75°F) until cream begins to thicken (12 to 16 hours). Refrigerate for at least 1 day before using. Add 1 teaspoon sugar and a dash nutmeg; beat until stiff. Makes about ¾ cup.

Papaya-Yogurt Mold

When you choose a papaya for this lime-accented fruit salad, look for one that is mostly golden for maximum ripeness. If the fruit is partly green, it will ripen at home at room temperature in 2 or 3 days—but for this to happen, the fruit should be at least a third golden when you buy it.

1 package (3 oz) orange-flavored gelatin
1¼ cups boiling water
1 cup orange yogurt
½ teaspoon grated lime rind
2 tablespoons lime or lemon juice
1 small papaya, peeled, seeded and diced (about 2 cups)
½ cup halved seedless grapes
¼ cup toasted slivered almonds
Butter or Boston lettuce

1. In a large bowl mix gelatin and boiling water, stirring until gelatin dissolves. Add yogurt, mixing until smooth and well combined. Mix in lime rind.
2. Refrigerate until mixture is almost firm. Meanwhile, mix lime juice with papaya and set aside.
3. Beat gelatin mixture with electric mixer until fluffy. Fold in papaya mixture, grapes, and almonds. Place in a 4½- to 5-cup mold and refrigerate until firm (3 to 4 hours).
4. Unmold and serve on a lettuce-lined plate.

Makes 6 servings.

Cantaloupe-Lime Mousse

This cooling combination of melon and lime is perfect for a sizzling day.

1 small cantaloupe (1¼-1½ lbs)
1 envelope unflavored gelatin
½ cup water
1 can (6 oz) frozen limeade concentrate
½ cup sour cream
Green food coloring (optional)
½ cup whipping cream
Mint leaves, for garnish

1. Cut melon is half; remove and discard seeds. Cut into 1-inch melon balls. You should have about 2 cups.

2. Sprinkle gelatin over water in a small pan; let stand 5 minutes. Place over medium heat, stirring until gelatin dissolves. Remove from heat.
3. Add limeade concentrate, stirring until melted; then gradually add sour cream, mixing until smooth. Add a drop or two of food coloring to tint a pale green, if you wish. Refrigerate, stirring occasionally, until syrupy.
4. Whip cream until stiff; fold gelatin mixture into cream; then fold in melon balls.
5. Place mixture in a 4-cup mold. Refrigerate until firm (2 to 3 hours).
6. Unmold onto a serving plate. Garnish with mint.

Make 6 servings.

Creamy Blueberry Salad

During blueberry season, this lavender salad is a rare treat, both in taste and in appearance. It makes a lovely lunch when coupled with piquant Lemon-Nut bread (page 48).

1 large package (6 oz) black cherry-flavored gelatin
2 cups boiling water
1 cup *each* plain yogurt and sour cream
¼ teaspoon ground ginger
2 teaspoons grated lemon rind
2 cups fresh blueberries
Mint sprigs and strawberries *or* sweet cherries, for garnish

1. In a large bowl mix gelatin and boiling water, stirring until gelatin dissolves.
2. Smoothly combine yogurt, sour cream, ginger, and lemon rind. Stir into gelatin mixture until well blended. Refrigerate, stirring occasionally, until mixture is slightly thickened and syrupy.
3. Fold blueberries into gelatin mixture. Pour into a 6-cup mold. Refrigerate until firm (4 to 6 hours).
4. Unmold onto a serving plate; garnish with mint and strawberries or cherries.

Makes 6 to 8 servings.

Luscious looking Creamy Blueberry Salad is lighter than it appears, as it is made with yogurt. Homemade lemon bread (page 48) is a good accompaniment.

Peach Melba Ring

For a tempting summer lunch, serve this creamy golden ring, which is punctuated with chopped fresh peaches. It is filled with cottage cheese and drizzled with a raspberry sauce. Try this salad ring with the blueberry muffins on page 48.

1 package (3 oz) lemon-flavored gelatin
1 cup boiling water
1 can (6 oz) frozen orange juice concentrate, thawed
½ cup sour cream
½ cup whipping cream, beaten until stiff
3 cups peeled, pitted, diced peaches
1 tablespoon lemon juice
2 cups cottage cheese
 Raspberry Sauce (recipe follows)

1. In a large bowl, mix gelatin and boiling water, stirring until gelatin dissolves. Stir in orange juice concentrate, then sour cream, mixing until well combined. Refrigerate, stirring occasionally, until mixture is slightly thickened and syrupy.
2. Fold in whipped cream. Mix peaches and lemon juice and fold into gelatin mixture.
3. Pour into a 6½-cup ring mold (about 9 inches in diameter). Refrigerate until firm (3 to 4 hours).
4. Unmold onto a serving plate. Fill center with cottage cheese. Drizzle with a little of the Raspberry Sauce. Serve remaining sauce in a bowl to add to individual servings at the table.

Makes 6 to 8 servings.

Raspberry Sauce

Thaw 1 package (10 oz) frozen raspberries. Purée in blender or food processor with 1 tablespoon sugar, 2 teaspoons lemon juice, and a dash of nutmeg until smooth; strain, if you wish, to remove seeds. Makes about 1 cup.

Welcome the first fresh summer peaches with golden Peach Melba Ring. Filled with cottage cheese, drizzled with a raspberry sauce, and accompanied by freshly baked blueberry muffins, the salad makes a perfect warm weather lunch.

Honeyed Boysenberry Yogurt Mold

This salad is simple to prepare and the plump fresh berries make the finished product a special treat. You can also make it with blackberries or olallieberries.

1 envelope unflavored gelatin
½ cup cold water
1 cup cottage cheese
1 cup plain yogurt
3 tablespoons honey
½ teaspoon *each* vanilla and grated lemon rind
1 tablespoon lemon juice
1½ cups boysenberries, olallieberries, *or* blackberries
 Leaf lettuce or watercress, for garnish

1. Sprinkle gelatin over cold water in a small saucepan. Let stand 5 minutes. Place over low heat; stir until gelatin dissolves. Remove from heat and cool slightly.
2. In blender or food processor, whirl or process cottage cheese with yogurt and honey until smooth and creamy.
3. In mixing bowl blend cottage cheese mixture, dissolved gelatin, vanilla, lemon rind, and lemon juice. Refrigerate, stirring occasionally, until mixture begins to thicken and becomes syrupy. Fold in berries.
4. Pour into a 4-cup mold. Refrigerate until firm (3 to 4 hours).
5. Unmold onto a serving plate; garnish with lettuce or watercress.

Makes 4 to 6 servings.

Frozen Summer Fruit Salad

There is no gelatin in this salad, but it is formed in shapely individual molds. The strawberries give it a sherbet-like quality. Unmolding each of the little salads requires only a very brief dip in hot water.

1 large nectarine (unpeeled), pitted and diced
1 cup halved, hulled fresh strawberries
2 tablespoons lemon juice
½ cup sugar
 Pinch nutmeg
1 package (3 oz) cream cheese, softened
1 teaspoon grated lemon rind
¼ cup halved seedless grapes
2 tablespoons toasted chopped almonds
 Whole strawberries, for garnish

1. Reserving ¼ cup *each* of the diced nectarine and halved strawberries, place remaining nectarine and strawberries in food processor or blender with lemon juice, sugar, nutmeg, and cream cheese. Process or whirl until smooth.
2. Fold in lemon rind, grapes, almonds, and reserved nectarine and strawberries. Divide mixture evenly into six ½-cup molds.
3. Cover each and freeze until firm (1 to 2 hours). Unmold onto plates. Let stand in refrigerator 15 to 30 minutes before serving. Garnish with whole strawberries.

Makes 6 servings.

Tangy Seafood Salad

Made with either medium-size shrimp or a combination of tiny shrimp and crabmeat, this creamy salad mold is an enticing choice for a cold buffet.

2 envelopes unflavored gelatin
1 cup cold water
¾ cup tomato juice
½ cup chili sauce
1 large package (8 oz) cream cheese
1 tablespoon prepared horseradish
1½ teaspoons Worcestershire sauce
½ teaspoon salt
½ cup *each* mayonnaise and sour cream
1 pound medium shrimp, shelled, deveined, and cooked (see page 75) (or ¼ pound *each* cooked crabmeat and small peeled, cooked shrimp)
1 green pepper, seeded and chopped
1 stalk celery, finely chopped
2 green onions, thinly sliced
Chicory, for garnish

1. Sprinkle gelatin over water in a small bowl; let stand 5 minutes.
2. Meanwhile, in a medium saucepan mix tomato juice and chili sauce. Add cream cheese, cut in chunks, and stir over medium heat until cheese melts and blends with tomato mixture. Add gelatin mixture, stirring until gelatin dissolves. Remove from heat and transfer to a large bowl. Mix in horseradish, Worcestershire sauce, and salt. Blend in mayonnaise and sour cream. Refrigerate, stirring occasionally, until mixture begins to thicken.
3. Stir in shrimp, green pepper, celery, and onions. Place in a 6-cup mold. Refrigerate until firm (4 to 5 hours).
4. Unmold onto a serving plate. Garnish with chicory sprigs.

Makes 6 servings.

Piquant Tuna Ring

Here is a hearty main dish salad that is satisfying for lunch or supper with toasted English muffins.

1 envelope unflavored gelatin
¾ cup water
1 can (8 oz) tomato sauce
¼ cup chili sauce
½ cup mayonnaise
¼ cup small macaroni shells
½ cup whipping cream
1 tablespoon prepared horseradish
Pinch cayenne pepper
1 can (6½ oz) chunk light tuna, drained and flaked
1 green onion, thinly sliced
1 stalk celery, finely chopped
¼ cup sliced stuffed green olives

1. Sprinkle gelatin over water in a small saucepan; let stand 5 minutes. Place over medium heat, stirring until gelatin dissolves. Transfer mixture to a mixing bowl.
2. To gelatin mixture add tomato sauce and chili sauce, mixing until well combined. Gradually add mayonnaise, mixing until smooth. Refrigerate, stirring occasionally, until mixture is slightly thickened and syrupy.
3. Cook macaroni according to package directions until tender; drain. Rinse with cold water and drain again.
4. Whip cream until stiff; blend in horseradish and cayenne. Fold cream into tomato mixture; then fold in cooked macaroni, tuna, green onion, celery, and olives. Spread mixture in a 5½-cup ring mold (about 8½ inches in diameter). Refrigerate until firm (3 to 4 hours).
5. Unmold onto a serving plate. Serve with additional mayonnaise, if you wish.

Makes 6 servings.

Crab and Spinach Loaf

This molded salad has a refreshing lightness. It is accompanied by a homemade mayonnaise flavored with capers.

1 envelope unflavored gelatin
6 tablespoons dry sherry
1 tablespoon *each* lemon juice and tomato paste
¼ teaspoon dried tarragon
⅓ cup mayonnaise
¾ cup cooked crabmeat, flaked (leave several pieces whole)
2 cups lightly packed fresh spinach leaves, shredded
3 green onions, thinly sliced
2 tablespoons chopped fresh parsley
2 eggs, separated
⅛ teaspoon salt
½ cup whipping cream
Spinach leaves, for garnish
Caper Mayonnaise (recipe follows)

1. Sprinkle gelatin over sherry in a small saucepan; let stand 5 minutes. Place over medium heat, stirring until gelatin dissolves. Remove from heat and mix in lemon juice, tomato paste, and tarragon. Gradually add mayonnaise, mixing until smooth.
2. In a large bowl mix crab, shredded spinach, green onions, and parsley. Beat egg whites with salt until stiff but not dry; set aside. Using same bowl and beaters, whip cream until stiff.
3. Lightly stir together gelatin mixture and crab mixture. Fold in whipped cream, then egg whites. Spread in an oiled 4½- by 8½-inch loaf pan.
4. Cover and refrigerate until firm (at least 3 hours). Unmold onto a serving plate and garnish with spinach leaves. Slice and accompany with Caper Mayonnaise.

Makes 6 to 8 servings.

Caper Mayonnaise

In blender or food processor combine 2 egg yolks (reserved from separated eggs in crab loaf), 1 tablespoon liquid from capers, 2 teaspoons Dijon mustard, ½ teaspoon salt, ¼ teaspoon paprika, 2 tablespoons tarragon wine vinegar, and ¼ cup olive oil. Cover and whirl or process for a few seconds. Then begin to add in a slow, steady stream ¾ cup salad oil. Whirl until thick and smooth. Transfer to a bowl and mix in 1 tablespoon drained capers. Makes about 1¼ cups.

Salmon Mousse

Fontina cheese lends a distinctive flavor to this molded cold salmon dish. Serve it as a first course or for a cold supper with French rolls and a chilled white wine such as Chardonnay.

2   salmon steaks (about 1½ lbs)
2   envelopes unflavored gelatin
½   cup water
2   tablespoons *each* butter or margarine and flour
1   teaspoon salt
½   teaspoon *each* paprika and dry mustard
    Dash cayenne pepper
2   cups milk
2   cups (½ lb) shredded fontina cheese
½   cup sour cream
¼   cup chopped fresh parsley
1   stalk celery, finely chopped
½   cup whipping cream
    Watercress *or* parsley sprigs and tomato wedges, for garnish
    Green Mayonnaise (see page 90), optional

1. Place salmon steaks on a rack over about ½ inch of water in a medium frying pan. Bring water to boiling, cover, reduce heat, and steam until salmon flakes when tested with a fork (10 to 12 minutes). Remove and discard skin and bones; flake salmon. Cover and refrigerate until ready to add to salad.
2. Sprinkle gelatin over water in a small bowl; let stand 5 minutes.
3. In a medium saucepan melt butter over medium heat. Mix in flour, salt, paprika, dry mustard, and cayenne; cook, stirring, until bubbly. Remove from heat. Gradually mix in milk until well blended. Cook, stirring constantly, until thickened and smooth. Add cheese and mix until melted. Add gelatin mixture, stirring until dissolved. Remove from heat.
4. Smoothly mix in sour cream; then add salmon. Refrigerate, stirring occasionally, until mixture begins to thicken.
5. Mix in parsley and celery. Beat cream until stiff; fold into gelatin mixture. Spread in an oiled 5-cup fish-shaped mold. Refrigerate until firm (at least 3 hours).
6. Unmold onto serving plate and garnish with watercress sprigs and tomatoes. Accompany with Green Mayonnaise, if you wish.

Makes 6 to 8 servings.

Creamy Egg Salad

To serve this salad as a main dish, add a plate of sliced cold meats; an assortment of olives, pickles, and radishes; light rye bread; and beer or iced tea.

1   envelope unflavored gelatin
¾   cup cold water
½   teaspoon *each* salt and curry powder
2   tablespoons lemon juice
1   tablespoon Dijon mustard
½   cup *each* mayonnaise and sour cream
1   stalk celery, thinly sliced
½   sweet red or green bell pepper, seeded and finely chopped
¼   cup chopped sweet pickles
5   hard-cooked eggs, chopped
    Red leaf lettuce

1. Sprinkle gelatin over water in a medium saucepan; let stand 5 minutes. Place over low heat and stir until gelatin dissolves; remove from heat.
2. Mix in salt, curry powder, lemon juice, mustard, mayonnaise, and sour cream, stirring with a whisk until mixture is smooth. Refrigerate, stirring occasionally, until mixture is slightly thickened and syrupy.
3. Mix in celery, green pepper, pickles, and eggs. Place in a 3½- to 4-cup mold. Refrigerate until firm (2 to 3 hours).
4. Unmold onto a lettuce-lined plate.

Makes 4 servings.

Warm Weather Supper

Cool foods, prepared ahead, are the answer to scorching weather. Here is a handsome assortment of refreshing foods, all suitable for a warm summer evening.

The chicken breasts for the main dish can be poached, glazed, and decorated as much as a day in advance. The dessert, a creamy sherbet, can be prepared and stored in the freezer as much as a week ahead, if you choose. Purchase cookies from a favorite bakery.

Creamy Glazed Chicken Breasts

3   whole chicken breasts, cut into 6 halves
1¼ cups water
½   cup dry white wine
¼   cup chopped onion
1   carrot, thinly sliced
1   sprig parsley
¼   teaspoon salt
    Pinch dried thyme
1½ teaspoons unflavored gelatin
2   teaspoons lemon juice
1   tablespoon Dijon mustard
⅓   cup *each* mayonnaise and sour cream
    Cherry tomato and pitted ripe olive slices and parsley sprigs, for decoration
    Shredded lettuce
    Hard-cooked egg wedges, whole cherry tomatoes, and ripe olives, for garnish

1. Place halved chicken breasts in a large frying pan. Add water, wine, onion, carrot, parsley, salt, and thyme. Bring to boiling, cover, reduce heat, and simmer until chicken is just tender (10 to 12 minutes). Remove and reserve chicken breasts.
2. Strain cooking liquid, discarding vegetables. Bring cooking liquid to boiling; boil vigorously until

liquid is reduced to ¾ cup. Let stand until cool.

3. Remove skin and bones from chicken breasts, leaving each in a neat whole piece; cover and refrigerate.

4. Sprinkle gelatin over reserved ¾ cup broth; let stand 5 minutes. Then heat, stirring until gelatin is dissolved. Remove from heat and smoothly mix in lemon juice, mustard, mayonnaise, and sour cream.

5. Dip each chicken breast into creamy gelatin mixture; then place on a rack over a shallow, rimmed baking sheet. Refrigerate chicken and remaining gelatin mixture just until gelatin begins to thicken. Spoon gelatin mixture evenly over chicken breasts to coat. Decorate each chicken breast with a cherry tomato slice, ripe olive slices, and parsley sprigs. Refrigerate until coating is firm (at least 1 hour).

6. Serve on a bed of shredded lettuce, garnished with hard-cooked eggs, cherry tomatoes, and ripe olives.

Makes 6 servings.

Pita Toast Parmesan

3 pita (pocket) breads
¼ cup butter or margarine
1 clove garlic, minced or pressed
⅛ teaspoon paprika
1 tablespoon chopped fresh parsley
2 tablespoons grated Parmesan cheese

1. Carefully separate each pita bread into two halves. Cut each half into quarters. Arrange in a single layer, insides up, on an ungreased baking sheet.

2. In a small pan melt butter over medium heat. Mix in garlic, paprika, and parsley. Brush butter mixture lightly over pita bread triangles. Sprinkle evenly with cheese.

3. Bake in a 350°F oven until crisp and golden brown (12 to 15 minutes). Serve warm.

Makes 6 servings.

This do-ahead dinner includes cold glazed chicken breasts, crisp triangles of pita bread, and a delicious berry sherbet.

Boysenberry Freeze

1 bag (1 lb) frozen boysenberries, thawed
1 cup sugar
2 tablespoons lemon juice
1 cup whipping cream

1. Place berries and their liquid in blender or food processor. Whirl or process until smooth. Add sugar and lemon juice and whirl or process again until well combined. Strain, if you wish, to remove seeds.

2. Whip cream until stiff. Fold in boysenberry mixture. Spread in an 8-inch-square pan and freeze until firm (about 2 hours).

3. Remove pan from freezer, break up berry mixture with a spoon, and transfer to a bowl. Beat until smooth. Pour into a freezer container, cover, and freeze again.

4. Let sherbet stand in refrigerator about 30 minutes before scooping into dishes to serve.

Makes about 1 quart.

Fruit Salads

If virtually any vegetable can be the starting point for a salad, the same can be said of fruits. From winter's tart and juicy citrus to summer's berries and cherries, fruits are salad bowl treasures.

New fresh fruits to inspire salads seem to appear every season. While few are actually new varieties, better transportation has made it possible to find more fruits from faraway lands. At one time fresh pineapple was a rare treat; now it is a year-round staple of most good produce markets. Tropical fruits such as papayas and mangoes are in ever better supply. The elegant kiwi fruit comes to us from both New Zealand and California.

In many respects fruits are more delicate than vegetables and leafy greens. This means that in handling them and preparing fruit salads you must be gentle. Sumptuously ripe fruits need a particularly light touch, from rinsing and peeling through cutting and mixing.

As a first course, side dish, or dessert, ⅔ to 1 cup of most fruit salads makes an adequate serving. Of course, if you are indulging in a handsome plate of fruit as a full meal, you can be more generous.

Red Pear Summer Salad

Red-skinned Bartlett pears are a summer treat. If they are firm when you buy them, for best flavor let them ripen at room temperature until they begin to soften. A cousin

Whatever the weather, you will find plenty of fruit for salads such as Ambrosia (page 42). Colorful Red Pear Summer Salad is shown at the right.

of the ever-popular Waldorf salad, this version has a gingery sour cream dressing and toasted almonds.

5   small red Bartlett pears
1   tablespoon lemon juice
2   cups seedless grapes
½   cup thinly sliced celery
½   cup toasted slivered almonds (see note)
     Creamy Ginger Dressing (recipe follows)
     Lettuce leaves

1. Core (but do not peel) and dice pears; you should have about 5 cups. Mix with lemon juice.
2. Add grapes and celery. Reserving 2 tablespoons of the almonds for garnish, add remaining almonds to fruit mixture. Mix lightly with dressing. Cover and refrigerate for 1 to 3 hours to blend flavors.
3. Serve salad in lettuce-lined bowl or on lettuce leaves on individual plates. Sprinkle with reserved almonds.

Makes 6 servings.

Note: To toast almonds, spread in a shallow pan. Bake in a 350°F oven until lightly browned (8 to 10 minutes).

Creamy Ginger Dressing

In a small bowl smoothly mix ⅓ cup *each* sour cream and mayonnaise, 2 tablespoons slivered preserved ginger, 1 teaspoon syrup from ginger, and a dash *each* ground allspice and dry mustard. Makes about ⅔ cup.

🍂 Autumn Fruit Salad Lunch

Invite friends to share this wholesome lunch. It is as colorful as a fall day, bright with frost-touched leaves.

A striking arrangement of seasonal fruits fans out from a fresh cranberry, apple, and orange relish. With it go individual almond-crusted cheese balls, to spread on whole wheat bread or crackers.

There is little last-minute work in this lunch; the relish, cheese balls, and homemade chocolate chip cake can all be prepared a day ahead.

Autumn Cranberry Relish Plates

1   pound fresh cranberries
2   medium-size tart apples (unpeeled), cored and cut in chunks
2   seedless oranges (unpeeled), cut in chunks
1   cup sugar
    Butter or Boston lettuce
6   small bunches red grapes
3   winter pears, halved and cored
3   bananas, cut diagonally into ½-inch slices
    Nippy Cheese Balls (recipe follows)
1   cup dates
    Lemon juice
    Mixed nuts in shells

1. Rinse and drain cranberries, removing any stems. Grind, using coarse blade of food chopper, with apples and oranges. Mix in sugar. Cover and refrigerate for several hours or overnight to blend flavors.
2. To serve, on each of 6 plates arrange lettuce leaves; spoon cranberry relish into center of each plate. Around relish on each plate arrange a bunch of grapes, a pear half, about 6 banana slices, a cheese ball, and a few dates. Brush bananas and pears with lemon juice. Add nuts, or serve in a separate bowl. Provide a nutcracker.
3. Serve salads at once.

Makes 6 servings.

Nippy Cheese Balls

Soften 1 package (3 oz) cream cheese. Mix in 1 cup shredded sharp Cheddar cheese, 1 teaspoon Dijon mustard, and a pinch of cayenne pepper. Shape into 6 balls. Roll them in ⅓ cup finely chopped toasted, salted, blanched almonds to coat thoroughly. Cover and refrigerate if made ahead. Makes 6.

Note: Recipe makes about 5 cups cranberry relish. Any not served for salad can be frozen for another meal.

Chocolate Chip Pound Cake

¾   cup butter or margarine, softened
1   cup sugar
1   teaspoon *each* grated orange peel and vanilla
4   eggs
2   cups all-purpose flour
1   teaspoon baking powder
½   teaspoon salt
½   cup milk
½   cup semisweet chocolate morsels
    Powdered sugar

1. Using an electric mixer, cream butter and sugar in a large bowl, beating until light and fluffy. Mix in orange peel and vanilla. Add eggs, one at a time, beating well after each addition.
2. Mix flour, baking powder, and salt. Add flour mixture to butter mixture alternately with milk, stirring with a spoon after each addition *just until blended.* Fold in chocolate. Spread in a lightly floured, greased 5- by 9-inch loaf pan.
3. Bake in a 325°F oven until a wooden pick inserted in center comes out clean (1 to 1¼ hours). Let stand in pan about 10 minutes; then turn out onto a rack to complete cooling.
4. Sift powdered sugar over the cake before slicing.

Makes 1 cake.

Autumn fruits form an edible still life of a salad, featuring fresh cranberry relish, and savory cheese balls to spread on bread or crackers.

Pear and Cheese Salad

Pears have an affinity for the flavor and buttery texture of many cheeses. This salad, with shreds of sharp Cheddar cheese and a tart yogurt dressing, makes the most of that quality. You can use summer Bartlett pears or a winter variety such as Anjou or Comice.

4   medium pears
1   tablespoon lemon juice
1   cup shredded sharp Cheddar cheese
1   stalk celery, thinly sliced
⅓   cup roasted sunflower seeds
    Yogurt Dressing (recipe follows)
    Lettuce leaves

1. Core (but do not peel) and dice pears; you should have about 5 cups. Mix with lemon juice.
2. Add cheese and celery. Reserving 2 tablespoons sunflower seeds for garnish, add remaining seeds to pear mixture. Mix lightly with dressing. Cover and refrigerate for 1 to 3 hours to blend flavors.
3. Serve salad in lettuce-lined bowl or on lettuce leaves on individual plates. Sprinkle with reserved sunflower seeds.

Makes 6 servings.

Yogurt Dressing
In a small bowl mix until smooth ⅓ cup plain yogurt, ¼ cup mayonnaise, 1 teaspoon Dijon mustard, ½ teaspoon grated lemon rind, and a dash ground allspice. Makes about ½ cup.

Orange Waldorf Salad

Orange juice and zesty orange rind give a lift to an enjoyable Waldorf salad with apples, grapes, and walnuts.

5   medium-size tart red-skinned apples
2   tablespoons orange juice
1½ cups halved, seeded red grapes
1   stalk celery, thinly sliced
½   cup coarsely chopped toasted walnuts (see note)
    Orange-Yogurt Dressing (recipe follows)
    Lettuce leaves
    Orange slices, for garnish

1. Core (but do not peel) and dice apples; you should have 5 to 6 cups. Mix with orange juice.
2. Add grapes, celery, and walnuts. Mix lightly with dressing. Cover and refrigerate for 1 to 3 hours to blend flavors.
3. Serve in a lettuce-lined bowl or on lettuce leaves on individual plates. Garnish with orange slices.

Makes 6 to 8 servings.

Note: To toast walnuts, spread in a shallow pan. Bake in a 350°F oven until lightly browned (8 to 10 min.).

Orange-Yogurt Dressing
In a small bowl mix ⅓ cup *each* plain yogurt and mayonnaise, 1 tablespoon *each* brown sugar and grated orange rind, and ⅛ teaspoon ground nutmeg until smooth. Makes about ⅔ cup.

Ambrosia Salad

Ambrosia is a southern dessert classic—a simple and elegant pairing of sliced oranges and a sprinkling of coconut. This luscious salad variation employs these elements and more: fresh pineapple, banana, and a whipped cream dressing. If you want to make it a little less sweet, use the unsweetened coconut available in natural foods stores.

Technique Tips — *Cutting Fruits*

Pineapple. With a long, sharp knife, cut fresh pineapple lengthwise through crown into halves or quarters. For maximum sweetness, choose fragrant, golden fruit – once picked, pineapple does not ripen or become appreciably more flavorful. Cut out fruit with a curved knife. Cut out end and core, then dice fruit into bite-size pieces. If you wish, use the hollowed-out pineapple "boat" to serve the fruit, alone or in other tempting salad combinations.

Papaya. For best flavor, be sure fresh papayas are fully ripe. Choose one that is at least half golden, then let it ripen at room temperature for 2 to 3 days. If papaya is to be peeled, use a vegetable parer to remove skin in thin slices. With a spoon, scoop out the shiny black seeds – Papaya and Avocado Salad on page 44 takes advantage of their peppery flavor for its dressing. Slice or dice the fruit, as recipe directs. Papaya halves also make handsome edible salad bowls.

3 seedless oranges, peeled and cut into bite-size pieces
2 cups diced fresh pineapple (or thawed frozen pineapple chunks, well drained)
1 banana, peeled and diced
1 tablespoon lemon juice
½ cup flaked coconut
½ cup whipping cream
1 tablespoon powdered sugar
¼ cup mayonnaise
   Lettuce leaves

1. Combine oranges and pineapple. Drizzle banana pieces with lemon juice; add to orange mixture. Sprinkle with coconut. Mix lightly. If made ahead, cover and refrigerate.
2. Shortly before serving, whip cream with powdered sugar until stiff; fold in mayonnaise. Fold dressing lightly into fruit mixture.
3. Serve at once in lettuce-lined bowl.

Makes 6 servings.

   Note: If you wish, you can add ½ cup miniature marshmallows to fruit mixture.

Citrus Cup with Fluffy Golden Dressing

Some fruit salads are as appealing as dessert as they are as a first-course fruit cup. This pretty citrus medley is one of those.

1 pink grapefruit
3 seedless oranges
2 cups diced fresh pineapple
¼ cup pomegranate seeds
   Fluffy Golden Dressing (recipe follows)

1. Peel grapefruit and oranges, dividing fruit into segments. Lightly mix grapefruit and orange segments and pineapple in a glass bowl. Cover and refrigerate for 1 to 3 hours to blend flavors.
2. Serve fruit in large serving bowl or individual dishes, sprinkled with pomegranate seeds. Accompany with dressing to spoon over each serving to taste.

Makes 6 servings.

Fluffy Golden Dressing
Beat 1 egg yolk with 1 tablespoon *each* honey and lemon juice and a pinch of nutmeg until thick and pale. Beat ⅓ cup whipping cream until stiff; then gradually beat in egg yolk mixture until fluffy and well combined. Serve at once. Makes about ¾ cup.

This striking citrus cup combines grapefruit, orange, and pineapple.

Minted Melon Medley

Bite-size spheres of varicolored melon make a refreshing salad for a warm day. The mint dressing is really a sugar syrup flavored with crème de menthe, so this dish could easily be served as a dessert.

½ small honeydew melon (2½ to 3 lbs)
1 medium cantaloupe (1¾ to 2 lbs)
1 small wedge (1½ to 2 lbs) watermelon
  Minted Dressing (recipe follows)
  Mint sprigs, for garnish

1. Remove seeds from melons; cut into 1-inch balls.
2. Place melon balls in a glass bowl. Pour on dressing and mix lightly. Cover and refrigerate for 2 to 3 hours to blend flavors.
3. Serve in a glass bowl, garnished with mint sprigs.

Makes 6 to 8 servings.

Minted Dressing

In a small pan mix ¼ cup sugar and 2 tablespoons water. Bring to boiling and boil, uncovered, for 1 minute. Remove from heat and stir in 2 tablespoons white crème de menthe. Let stand until cool. Makes about ⅓ cup.

Papaya and Avocado Salad

Although avocados are usually served as a vegetable, like tomatoes they are technically a fruit. They are delicious in combination with sliced papaya and marinated tiny shrimp in this first-course salad. The dressing is speckled with peppery bits of papaya seed.

1 ripe papaya
½ cup salad oil
2 tablespoons tarragon wine vinegar
1 tablespon lime or lemon juice
¼ teaspoon *each* salt and dry mustard
1 green onion, thinly sliced
¼ pound small peeled, cooked shrimp
1 medium avocado, halved and pitted
  Butter or Boston lettuce leaves

1. Peel, halve, and scoop out seeds from papaya, reserving 2 teaspoons of the seeds. Slice papaya thinly; set aside.
2. In blender or food processor combine oil, vinegar, lime juice, salt, and dry mustard; whirl or process until well combined. Add reserved 2 teaspoons papaya seeds; whirl or process again until seeds are the consistency of coarsely ground pepper.
3. Pour dressing into a medium bowl; mix lightly with onion and shrimp.
4. Cut avocado into small balls, using a melon ball cutter; mix lightly with shrimp mixture.
5. Arrange lettuce on each of 4 salad plates. Place a fourth of the papaya slices on each. Spoon shrimp-avocado mixture over papaya, and top with any dressing remaining in bowl.

Makes 4 servings.

Honeydew, cantaloupe and watermelon mingle in the cool minted salad at left. The flavors are enhanced by a crème de menthe dressing.

Peppered Peach Salad

The sweet juiciness of peaches is surprisingly enhanced by a peppery red wine vinegar dressing, making a handsome first-course salad. Wreath the fruit in sprigs of watercress.

4 large peaches *or* nectarines (see note)
   Peppery Red Wine Vinaigrette Dressing (recipe follows)
   Watercress sprigs *or* chicory
   Snipped chives, for garnish (optional)

1. Halve peaches, peel, and remove seeds. Slice about ¼ inch thick.
2. Mix peach slices lightly with dressing; cover and refrigerate for 30 minutes to 1 hour to blend flavors.
3. Serve peaches on watercress or chicory, spooning dressing over. Sprinkle with chives, if you wish.

Makes 4 to 6 servings.

   Note: If nectarines are used, it is not necessary to peel them.

Peppery Red Wine Vinaigrette Dressing

In a small bowl mix 2 tablespoons red wine vinegar, ¼ teaspoon salt, ⅛ teaspoon coarsely ground black pepper, and a pinch of dried summer savory. Using a whisk or fork, gradually beat in ¼ cup salad oil until well combined.
Makes about 6 tablespoons.

Polynesian Banana Salad

This pretty salad can be served either as a first course or as a side dish with fried chicken, broiled lamb chops, or salmon.

½ medium cucumber
2 oranges
   Leaf lettuce
2 bananas
1 tablespoon lemon or lime juice
   Chutney Dressing (recipe follows)

1. Score cucumber (see page 17); slice thinly. Peel oranges; slice crosswise about ¼ inch thick.
2. On each of 4 lettuce-lined salad plates, arrange cucumber and orange slices in a circle around edge of plate. Peel and slice bananas on the diagonal, ½ inch thick. Mix lightly with lemon juice. Mound banana slices in center of cucumber-orange arrangement.
3. Drizzle dressing lightly over each serving. Serve remaining dressing in a bowl to add to taste.

Makes 4 servings.

Chutney Dressing

In a blender or food processor combine ⅓ cup *each* mayonnaise and sour cream, ¼ cup Major Grey—type chutney, 1 tablespoon lemon juice, ¼ teaspoon *each* salt and curry powder, and a pinch of cayenne pepper. Whirl or process until smooth. Makes about 1 cup.

There is a taste of the South Seas in this delightful fruit and vegetable salad with its creamy chutney dressing.

Avocado and Cantaloupe Salad

The accent of lime juice and rind gives this pretty salad a Mexican touch. To make it a more substantial first course, add one or two rolled slices of prosciutto or Black Forest ham to each serving.

½ medium cantaloupe (1¾ to 2 lbs)
1 large avocado
Butter or Boston lettuce
Lime Dressing (recipe follows)
Grated lime rind, for garnish

1. Scoop out and discard cantaloupe seeds. Peel and slice into thin crescents.
2. Halve, remove seed, and peel avocado. Thinly slice lengthwise.

3. Alternate cantaloupe and avocado slices on lettuce leaves on serving plate or 4 individual salad plates. Drizzle with dressing. Sprinkle with lime rind and serve at once.
Makes 4 servings.

Lime Dressing

In a small bowl mix 2 tablespoons lime juice, ¼ teaspoon salt, ⅛ teaspoon dry mustard, and a pinch of cayenne pepper. Using a whisk or fork, gradually beat in 1 tablespoon almond oil and 3 tablespoons salad oil (or omit almond oil and use ¼ cup salad oil) until well combined. Makes about 6 tablespoons.

Technique Tips — *Cutting Fruits*

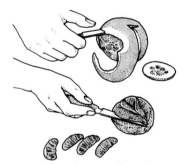

Oranges and Grapefruit. *To peel an orange or grapefruit, cut off one end; then peel close to fruit, cutting away any of the bitter white inner peel. Use a sharp paring knife and cut close to membranes, removing juicy segments of fruit for salads or desserts.*

Citrus stripper. *This tool makes long, threadlike strands of lemon, lime, or orange zest. Look for it in cutlery or gourmet cookware stores. The citrus shreds are not only a handsome garnish, they add aroma and flavor if freshly cut.*

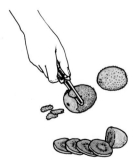

Kiwi Fruit. *Fuzzy, brownish kiwi fruit has a curious looking surface appearance, but inside it is beautiful. Use a vegetable peeler to remove skin. Slice fruit about 1/4-inch thick. The interior is apple-green, with a ring of tiny, edible black seeds.*

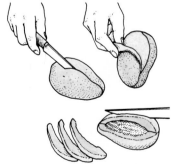

Mangoes. *To peel a juicy, fresh mango, first cut around the circumference from end to end. Peel back the skin as you would a banana. Fruit tends to cling to the large, fuzzy seed – cut slices away from this seed as you would with a cling peach.*

Spring Fruit Salad with Orange Dressing

Each season has its irresistible fresh fruits. This main dish luncheon combination sings of spring.

Leaf lettuce
1 small pineapple (2 lbs), peeled, cored, and cut in long, thin wedges
1 small cantaloupe (1¼ to 1½ lbs), cut in half lengthwise, seeded, peeled, and cut into 6 to 8 wedges
1 basket (2 to 3 cups) strawberries
4 to 6 small bunches seedless grapes
2 cups cottage cheese
Fluffy Orange Dressing (recipe follows)

1. On lettuce leaves on individual chilled plates arrange pineapple and cantaloupe wedges, strawberries (with hulls), and grapes around a mound of cottage cheese.
2. Serve with a bowl of Orange Dressing to spoon over each serving.

Makes 4 to 6 servings.

Fluffy Orange Dressing

Beat 1 cup whipping cream until stiff. Fold in ⅛ teaspoon ground nutmeg, ¼ cup thawed frozen orange juice concentrate, and ¼ cup mayonnaise. Chill for 1 to 2 hours to blend flavors. Makes about 2½ cups.

Tropical Fruit Bowl

Here is another salad that can either begin or end a meal. It combines a variety of somewhat exotic fruits in a gingered honey-rum syrup.

2 cups diced fresh pineapple
1 medium papaya, peeled, seeded, and diced (see page 42)
1 mango or peach, peeled, seeded, and sliced
1 kiwi fruit, peeled and cut in ¼-inch-thick rounds
Honey-Rum Dressing (recipe follows)
2 bananas, peeled and sliced on the diagonal, ½ inch thick

1. Lightly mix pineapple, papaya, mango, kiwi fruit, and their juices

with dressing in a large bowl. Cover and refrigerate 2 to 3 hours.

2. Mix in bananas and serve immediately in a glass bowl.

Makes 6 servings.

Honey-Rum Dressing

To ¼ cup honey in a small bowl, gradually add 2 tablespoons rum and 1 tablespoon lime juice, then ⅛ teaspoon ground ginger. Mix until well blended. Makes about ½ cup.

Red Fruit Plate with Cream Cheese Dressing

A jewel box of summer fruits, ranging in color from pink through crimson to Burgundy red, makes an eye-catching summer salad arrangement. Even the dressing — cream cheese, whipped cream, and a touch of plum jam — has a pink blush.

> Red leaf lettuce
> Cream Cheese Dressing
> (recipe follows)

1 cup sweet cherries with stems

1 basket (2 to 3 cups) strawberries

8 figs, sliced crosswise

4 wedges (about 1½ in. thick) watermelon

2 nectarines, pitted and cut in wedges

4 red plums, halved and pitted

1 bunch (about 1 lb) red seedless grapes

1. Line 4 plates with lettuce. At one side or in center of each, place a dollop or a small bowl of dressing.

2. Divide fruits among the 4 plates, arranging them attractively with red surfaces up.

Makes 4 servings.

Cream Cheese Dressing

Soften 1 package (3 oz) cream cheese; beat until creamy. Gradually beat in 1 tablespoon lemon juice, 2 tablespoons plum jam, and ¾ cup whipping cream until thick. Refrigerate for about 1 hour to blend flavors. Makes about 1½ cups.

Red Fruit Plates are a spectrum of reds, oranges, and pinks. The Orange Sugar Biscuits on page 49 are a good accompaniment for this fruit salad lunch.

Breads to Bake for Salads

The cool crispness of a salad main dish seems to call for a luscious, freshly baked bread as a complement. Here are five suggestions, each one special.

Moist Lemon-Nut Bread

Sweetly lemon saturated, this quick loaf develops flavor as it stands (wrapped airtight) overnight.

½   cup (¼ lb) butter or margarine, softened
1   cup sugar
    Grated rind of 1 lemon
2   eggs
1¼ cups all-purpose flour
1   teaspoon baking powder
¼   teaspoon salt
⅛   teaspoon ground mace or nutmeg
½   cup milk
½   cup finely chopped pecans or walnuts
    Lemon Syrup (recipe follows)

1. Cream butter and sugar until fluffy. Beat in lemon rind; then add eggs, one at a time, beating well after each addition.
2. Mix flour, baking powder, salt, and mace. Add flour mixture to butter mixture alternately with milk, mixing after each addition just until blended. Fold in nuts. Spread batter in a well-greased 4½- by 8½-inch loaf pan.
3. Bake in a 350°F oven until bread is well browned and center tests done when a long wooden pick is inserted (45 to 55 minutes).
4. Remove pan to a wire rack and pierce bread all over with a small skewer. Pour Lemon Syrup evenly over hot bread. Let cool in pan for about 30 minutes; then turn out and complete cooling on rack. Slice thinly when cool. Makes 1 loaf.

Lemon Syrup

Squeeze juice from 1 lemon. (You should have 3 to 4 tablespoons.) Heat in a small pan until lukewarm; stir in ¼ cup sugar until dissolved.

Blueberry-Lemon Muffins

You can bake these sugar-sprinkled muffins with fresh blueberries or with un-sweetened frozen ones. (If using the latter, the berries should be frozen when you stir them into the batter.)

2   cups all-purpose flour
1   tablespoon baking powder
½   teaspoon *each* salt and ground nutmeg
⅓   cup sugar
1   egg
1   cup milk
3   tablespoons salad oil
2   teaspoons grated lemon rind
1   tablespoon lemon juice
1   cup blueberries, fresh or frozen

1. In a medium bowl mix flour, baking powder, salt, ¼ teaspoon of the nutmeg, and ¼ cup of the sugar. Mix remaining ¼ teaspoon nutmeg with remaining 1⅓ tablespoons sugar in a small bowl; set aside.
2. In a small bowl beat egg with milk, salad oil, lemon rind, and lemon juice. Add egg mixture to flour mixture all at once; mix just until combined. Fold in blueberries.
3. Divide mixture evenly into 12 greased 2½-inch muffin cups; sprinkle nutmeg-sugar mixture evenly over muffins. Bake in a 425°F oven until golden brown (18 to 20 minutes). Makes 1 dozen.

Quick Orange-Pecan Sticky Buns

A faster version of the popular yeast rolls, this delicious bread goes well with a main dish fruit salad.

⅔   cup butter or margarine
½   cup firmly packed light brown sugar
½   cup coarsely chopped pecans
2   tablespoons grated orange rind
2   cups all-purpose flour
1   tablespoon baking powder
½   teaspoon salt
⅔   cup half-and-half (light cream)
3   tablespoons granulated sugar

1. Melt ¼ cup of the butter in a 9-inch-round baking pan. Sprinkle evenly with brown sugar, pecans, and 1 table-spoon of the orange rind.
2. Thoroughly mix flour, baking powder, and salt in a medium bowl. Cut in ¼ cup of the remaining butter until coarse crumbs form. Add half-and-half all at once, mixing gently just until a soft dough forms. Turn dough out onto a lightly floured board or pastry cloth. Knead gently 30 sec-onds. Roll out into an 8- by 13-inch rectangle.
3. Melt remaining 2⅔ table-spoons butter; brush over dough, leaving a ½-inch mar-gin on one long side. Mix granulated sugar and remain-ing 1 tablespoon orange rind; sprinkle over butter. Roll up dough like a jelly roll, begin-ning at long side opposite margin. Moisten edge and seal. Cut into 12 equal slices. Place rolls, cut side down, in pre-pared pan.
4. Bake in a 425°F oven until rolls are well browned (20 to 25 minutes). Let stand about 30 seconds; then invert onto serv-ing plate. Makes 1 dozen.

Orange Sugar Biscuits

Crusty with orange sugar, these rich biscuits should probably be designated scones. They are best when warm.

¼ cup sugar
4 teaspoons grated orange rind
2 cups all-purpose flour
1 tablespoon baking powder
½ teaspoon salt
½ cup (¼ lb) firm butter or margarine
1 egg
½ cup half-and-half (light cream)
Half-and-half, for brushing

1. Mix sugar and orange rind in a mixing bowl; remove and set aside 1 tablespoon of the mixture.
2. To sugar mixture remaining in bowl add flour, baking powder, and salt. Mix to combine dry ingredients thoroughly. Cut in butter until coarse crumbs form.
3. Beat egg with the ½ cup half-and-half. Add egg mixture, all at once, to flour mixture; mix gently just until a soft dough forms. Turn dough out onto a floured board or pastry cloth, turning to coat lightly with flour. Pat or roll out about ½ inch thick. Cut into 2½-inch rounds. Place on an ungreased baking sheet. Brush tops lightly with half-and-half; sprinkle with reserved orange sugar.
4. Bake in a 425°F oven until golden (12 to 15 minutes). Serve warm.
Makes 1 dozen.

Sprouted Wheat-Berry Bread

Whole-grain goodness makes these crusty, moist-textured loaves a perfect choice with a hearty vegetable salad—or for bacon, lettuce, and tomato sandwiches.

¼ cup warm water
1 package active dry yeast
2 cups milk, scalded and cooled to lukewarm
¼ cup honey
1 tablespoon salt
2 tablespoons salad oil
4½ to 5 cups unbleached all-purpose flour
1 cup whole wheat *or* graham flour
1 cup sprouted wheat berries (see page 21)

1. Place warm water in a large bowl; sprinkle with yeast. Let stand until softened (3 to 5 minutes). Mix in milk, honey, salt, oil, 3 cups of the unbleached flour, and whole wheat flour. Mix to blend; then beat until dough is elastic and pulls away from sides of bowl (about 5 minutes).
2. Stir in sprouted wheat berries and 1 cup more of the unbleached flour to make a soft dough. Turn dough out onto a board or pastry cloth floured with some of the remaining ½ to 1 cup unbleached flour. Knead, adding more flour if dough is sticky, until dough is smooth and springy, with small bubbles just under surface (about 20 minutes).
3. Place dough in greased bowl; turn to grease top. Cover and let rise in a warm place until doubled (about 1½ hours). Punch dough down. Divide in half.
4. Shape each half into a loaf. Place loaves in greased 4½- by 8½- inch loaf pans. Let rise until nearly doubled (about 1 hour).
5. Bake in a 350°F oven until loaves are well browned and sound hollow when tapped (40 to 45 minutes).
Makes 2 loaves.

Clockwise from top left are blueberry muffins, orange biscuits, lemon bread, sprouted wheat bread, and sticky buns.

Potato, Rice, Bean, and Pasta Salads

Imagine the perfect picnic—a lazy day, blue skies, fried chicken. But what would it be without a bowl brimming with potato salad!

Potato salad and such hearty relatives as salads featuring pasta, rice, and beans or other legumes are always popular for picnics and other outings, barbecues, and for their filling qualities in winter meals.

When you plan to make a salad of this type, allow plenty of time. Most can be made, completely or in part, as much as a day ahead of serving. The major ingredients of these salads tend to be fairly bland in flavor, so allow time for seasonings to penetrate their recesses.

For a successful potato (or pasta, rice, or bean) salad, remember: The more surface area exposed, the more delicious the result. Cut potatoes in fairly small, bite-size pieces, just large enough so they will not crumble or become mushy when mixed with dressing. Small, hollow forms of pasta with lots of nooks and crannies will taste better in a salad than large, thick, smooth varieties.

Also, warm food absorbs flavors better than cold food does. When possible, add an assertively seasoned oil-and-vinegar dressing to cooked potatoes while they are still warm. Refrigerate the mixture until it is cold; then add crisp ingredients and a creamy dressing, if you like.

Dressings for potato, pasta, rice, and bean salads can be bolder than those for most other salads. Let your taste be your guide, but don't be surprised if you find yourself using salt, garlic, and herbs with a more generous hand than usual. Although the traditional proportions for an oil-and-vinegar dressing are three parts oil to one of vinegar, for a potato salad or its cousins, two parts oil to one of vinegar is not usually excessive.

During warm weather potato and pasta salads with creamy dressings need special care. Mayonnaise, eggs, meat, and milk products are hospitable media for bacterial growth; unless kept refrigerated, they can cause food-borne illnesses. Salads containing such ingredients should be kept cold. If the salad is to stand in a warm place for some time, place the bowl on ice. Use an insulated container to take the salad from your refrigerator to the picnic.

Well-made pasta, rice, and bean salads offer an abundance of flavor. Pesto and Noodle Salad (left and page 55) boasts a vivid fresh basil dressing. The potato salad at right (recipe, page 52) is golden with mustard.

🍂 Potato Salads

Golden Potato Salad

Creamy and delicious, this potato salad is a classic of its kind.

4   large smooth-skinned potatoes (2 to 2½ lbs)
    Salted water
3   tablespoons sherry wine vinegar
½   teaspoon salt
    Dash white pepper
1   small clove garlic, minced or pressed
¼   cup salad oil
¼   cup *each* chopped sweet pickles and sliced green onions
1   small green pepper, seeded and finely chopped
3   hard-cooked eggs, sliced
    Mustard Dressing (recipe follows)
    Lettuce leaves
    Radish roses and chopped parsley, for garnish

1. Cook potatos (unpeeled) in boiling salted water to cover until tender (35 to 40 minutes). Drain and, while warm, slip off skins and cut potatoes into ¾-inch cubes. (You should have about 6 cups.) Place in a large bowl.
2. While potatoes cook, in a small bowl mix vinegar, salt, pepper, and garlic. Using a whisk or fork, gradually beat in oil until well combined. Pour oil mixture over warm potatoes, stirring gently to coat all potatoes. Cover and refrigerate for at least 2 hours (or as long as overnight).
3. Lightly mix in pickles, green onions, green pepper, eggs, and dressing. Cover and refrigerate for 1 to 3 hours.
4. Serve in a lettuce-lined bowl. Garnish with radishes and parsley.

Makes 6 to 8 servings.

Mustard Dressing

Mix until smooth ⅓ cup *each* mayonnaise and sour cream, 1½ tablespoons prepared mustard, 1 teaspoon prepared horseradish, ¼ teaspoon celery seeds, and ¼ teaspoon salt. If you like a yellower color, blend in 1 to 2 drops yellow food coloring. Makes about ¾ cup.

Red-and-White Potato Salad

Here is a recipe for potato salad purists: tiny red potatoes, cooked and served in their jackets, crisp with radishes and green onions and enlivened by a hint of dill.

2   pounds (about 12) small new red potatoes
    Salted water
¼   cup red wine vinegar
1   tablespoon Dijon mustard
½   teaspoon salt
¼   teaspoon dried dill weed
⅛   teaspoon seasoned pepper
1   clove garlic, minced or pressed
½   cup salad oil
1   cup sliced radishes
6   green onions, thinly sliced
¼   cup chopped fresh parsley
¼   cup *each* mayonnaise and sour cream
    Hard-cooked egg wedges, for garnish

1. Cook potatoes (unpeeled) in boiling salted water to cover until tender (25 to 30 minutes). Drain and slice while warm. (You should have about 6 cups.) Place in a large bowl.
2. While potatoes cook, in a small bowl mix vinegar, mustard, salt, dill weed, seasoned pepper, and garlic. Using a whisk or fork, gradually beat in oil until well combined. Pour oil mixture over warm potatoes, stirring gently to coat slices. Cover and refrigerate for at least 2 hours (or as long as overnight, if you wish).
3. Gently mix in radishes, green onions, and parsley. Blend mayonnaise and sour cream until smooth; fold into potatoes. Cover and refrigerate for 1 to 3 hours. Garnish with egg wedges.

Makes 6 servings.

Curried Potato Salad

If it's color you want in a potato salad, try this one as a companion to chicken or pork.

1½ pounds (about 9) small new potatoes
   Salted water
3 tablespoons cider vinegar
1 tablespoon lemon juice
2 teaspoons curry powder
1 teaspoon *each* mustard seeds, coarsely crushed, and salt
½ teaspoon grated lemon rind
1 clove garlic, minced or pressed
½ cup salad oil
5 green onions, thinly sliced
1 jar (2 oz) sliced pimientos, drained
1 stalk celery, finely chopped
½ cup thawed frozen peas
   Green leaf lettuce

1. Cook potatoes (unpeeled) in boiling salted water to cover until tender (25 to 30 minutes). Drain and slice while warm. (You should have about 6 cups.) Place in a large bowl.
2. While potatoes cook, in a medium bowl mix vinegar, lemon juice, curry powder, mustard seeds, salt, lemon rind, and garlic. In a small pan swirl oil over medium heat until it is just warm to touch (2 to 3 minutes). Using a whisk or fork, gradually beat hot oil into vinegar mixture until well combined.
3. Pour about half the dressing over warm potatoes, stirring gently to coat slices. Cover and refrigerate for at least 2 hours (or as long as overnight, if you wish).
4. Gently mix in green onions, pimientos, celery, and peas. Add remaining dressing and mix lightly. Cover and refrigerate for 1 to 3 hours. Serve in a lettuce-lined bowl.

Makes 4 to 6 servings.

Dill piques the flavor of this classic Red-and-White Potato Salad, made with new potatoes in their jackets. It will be a popular contribution to a cooperative picnic or summer potluck supper. To ensure freshness, keep it cold until time to serve.

Crispy Potato Salad with Blue Cheese

So many crisp, raw vegetables are combined in this salad that it seems somehow healthier than one expects a potato salad to be. It is especially good with barbecued lamb.

1½ pounds (about 9) small new potatoes
   Salted water
3 tablespoons tarragon wine vinegar
2 teaspoons Dijon mustard
1 teaspoon salt
⅛ teaspoon *each* dried marjoram and white pepper
1 clove garlic, minced or pressed
⅓ cup salad oil
½ cup *each* sliced radishes and chopped cucumber
1 small onion, chopped
1 small green pepper, seeded and chopped
1 medium carrot, shredded
1 stalk celery, finely chopped
¼ cup chopped fresh parsley
2 hard-cooked eggs, sliced
¼ cup *each* mayonnaise, sour cream *or* plain yogurt, and crumbled blue-veined cheese
   Tomato wedges, for garnish

1. Cook potatos (unpeeled) in boiling salted water to cover until tender (25 to 30 minutes). Drain and slice while warm. (You should have about 6 cups.) Place in a large bowl.
2. While potatoes cook, in a small bowl mix vinegar, mustard, salt, marjoram, pepper, and garlic. Using a whisk or fork, gradually beat in oil until well combined. Pour oil mixture over warm potatoes, stirring gently to coat potato slices. Cover and refrigerate for at least 2 hours (or as long as overnight, if you wish).
3. Lightly mix in radishes, cucumber, onion, green pepper, carrot, celery, parsley, and hard-cooked eggs. Mix mayonnaise and sour cream until smooth; stir in cheese. Fold mayonnaise mixture into potatoes. Cover and refrigerate for 1 to 3 hours. Garnish with tomato wedges.

Makes 6 to 8 servings.

Winter Potato Salad with Fresh Fennel

This spicy salad makes a welcome addition to a winter meal of crisply pan-fried Italian sausages or smoked pork chops. Slivers of fresh fennel contribute a licorice-like flavor. This vegetable is also known by its Italian name, *finocchio*.

It looks like a short, stout bunch of celery, with a rounded bulb, short stalks, and feathery leaves. You will find it from September through April in stores where people of Italian descent shop. If you are unable to find it, substitute an equal amount of celery, and coarsely crush ¼ teaspoon fennel or anise seeds into the dressing.

4 medium-size smooth-skinned potatoes (about 2 lbs)
   Salted water
¼ cup sherry wine vinegar
1 clove garlic, minced or pressed
1 teaspoon *each* salt and sugar
¼ teaspoon ground allspice
¼ teaspoon whole white or black peppercorns, coarsely crushed
⅓ cup salad oil
¼ cup finely chopped onion
1 cup thinly sliced fresh fennel

1. Cook potatoes (unpeeled) in boiling salted water to cover until tender (35 to 40 minutes). Drain and, while warm, slip off skins; quarter potatoes and slice them about ¼ inch thick. (You should have about 6 cups.) Place in a large bowl.
2. While potatoes cook, in a small bowl mix vinegar, garlic, salt, sugar, allspice, and peppercorns. Using a whisk or fork, gradually beat in oil until well combined.
3. Pour about half of the dressing over potatoes. Add onion and mix lightly. Cover and refrigerate for at least 2 hours (or as long as overnight, if you wish).
4. Lightly mix in fennel and remaining dressing. Refrigerate until cold.

Makes 6 servings.

The ideal beverage to accompany this hot potato salad for supper is cold beer.

Hot Potato and Sausage Salad

Here is a potato salad that is really a full meal in one bowl. Serve the hot salad with beer and your favorite rye bread. If you buy Polish sausage that is not precooked, cover the sausage with boiling water and simmer gently 15 minutes before slicing and browning.

5 medium-size smooth-skinned potatoes (about 2 lbs)
   Salted water
1 pound Polish sausage (*kielbasa*), sliced about ¼ inch thick
2 tablespoons olive oil
1 medium onion, finely chopped
1 medium green pepper, seeded and thinly sliced
1 clove garlic, minced or pressed
⅓ cup *each* red wine vinegar and beef *or* chicken broth
1 teaspoon salt
⅛ teaspoon seasoned pepper
   Chopped parsley, for garnish

1. Cook potatoes (unpeeled) in boiling salted water to cover until tender (25 to 35 minutes). Drain; as soon as they are cool enough to handle, slip off skins. Cut potatoes into ½-inch-thick, bite-size pieces. Place in a deep warm bowl.
2. Cook sausage slices, stirring frequently, in heated oil in a large frying pan until lightly browned; remove with a slotted spoon and add to potatoes. To fat remaining in pan add onion and green pepper, stirring over medium heat for about 2 minutes. Mix in garlic, vinegar, broth, salt, and pepper. Cook until mixture boils, stirring to loosen sausage drippings. Boil 1 minute.
3. Pour green pepper mixture over potatoes and mix lightly. Sprinkle with parsley. Serve hot.

Makes 4 to 6 servings.

Pasta Salads

Tuna and Shells Salad

If you like, this salad can be a main dish for a warm weather lunch or supper. Add a basket of crisp crackers and some plump deviled eggs.

8 ounces (about 2 cups) small macaroni shells
1 can (6½ oz) chunk light tuna, drained and flaked
½ cup (2 oz) diced teleme or Monterey jack cheese (about ¼-inch cubes)
1 cup halved cherry tomatoes
1 stalk celery, thinly sliced
2 green onions, thinly sliced
¼ cup chopped fresh parsley
   Garlic-Basil Dressing (recipe follows)
   Leaf lettuce

1. Cook macaroni shells according to package directions. Drain, rinse with cold water, and drain again.
2. Mix shells lightly with tuna, cheese, cherry tomatoes, celery, green onions, parsley, and dressing. Cover and refrigerate for 1 hour or longer to blend flavors. Serve on lettuce leaves.

Makes 4 to 6 servings.

Garlic-Basil Dressing

In a small bowl mix 2 tablespoons *each* balsamic and red wine vinegar (or ¼ cup red wine vinegar), 1 teaspoon dried basil, ½ teaspoon salt, ¼ teaspoon *each* sugar and dried oregano, ⅛ teaspoon coarsely ground pepper, and 2 cloves garlic (minced or pressed). Using a whisk or fork gradually blend in 3 tablespoons olive oil and ⅓ cup salad oil until well combined. Makes about ⅔ cup.

The pasta salad shown at right features spiral egg noodles (sometimes called rotelle *or* fusilli) *with crisp, colorful vegetables. It is a sprightly addition to a supper featuring sliced cold meats or cold fried or roast chicken.*

Sweet-Sour Macaroni Salad

This creamy salad with a luscious chutney dressing is a fine companion to roast turkey or barbecued spareribs.

8   ounces (about 1¾ cups) salad macaroni
½   cup mayonnaise
¼   cup sour cream
1   tablespoon *each* sugar and cider vinegar
¼   cup Major Grey – type chutney (snipped to cut up large pieces of fruit)
1   stalk celery, finely chopped
½   cup diced baked ham
1   small jar (2 oz) diced pimientos, drained
    Chopped parsley, for garnish

1. Cook macaroni according to package directions. Drain, rinse with cold water, and drain again. Set aside.
2. For dressing, in a large bowl mix mayonnaise, sour cream, sugar, vinegar, and chutney until smooth.
3. To dressing add macaroni, celery, ham, and pimientos. Mix lightly to coat all ingredients with dressing. Cover and refrigerate for 1 hour or longer to blend flavors. Sprinkle with chopped parsley.

Makes 4 to 6 servings.

Pesto and Noodle Salad

Bow-tie noodles (also called *farfalle* or butterflies) are a good vehicle for a vividly colored and flavored basil-and-garlic dressing. You might serve this salad with quickly sautéed shrimp or with an herbed roast chicken.

8   ounces (about 3 cups) medium-size noodle bows
3   tablespoons red wine vinegar
1   tablespoon dried basil (or ½ cup lightly packed fresh basil leaves)
¼   cup chopped fresh parsley
2   cloves garlic, minced or pressed
½   teaspoon salt
¼   teaspoon sugar
⅓   cup grated Parmesan cheese
½   cup olive oil or salad oil
    Freshly ground pepper
    Cherry tomatoes, for garnish

1. Cook noodle bows according to package directions. Drain, rinse with cold water, and drain again.
2. In blender or food processor combine vinegar, basil (if fresh basil is used, omit parsley), parsley, garlic, salt, sugar, Parmesan cheese, and olive oil. Whirl or process until smooth and well combined.
3. Lightly mix noodle bows and dressing. Cover and refrigerate for 1 hour or longer to blend flavors. Serve sprinkled with pepper and garnished with cherry tomatoes.

Makes 4 to 6 servings.

Noodle Twist Salad

To accompany an assortment of sliced cold meats or chicken, serve this sprightly and colorful salad.

8   ounces (about 3 cups) spiral egg noodles
½   cup *each* slivered ripe olives and thawed frozen peas
1   medium-size red onion, thinly sliced and separated into rings
1   sweet red or green bell pepper, seeded and chopped
¼   cup chopped fresh parsley
    Caper Dressing (recipe follows)

1. Cook noodles according to package directions. Drain, rinse with cold water, and drain again.
2. Mix noodles lightly with olives, peas, onion, red pepper, parsley, and dressing. Cover and refrigerate for 1 hour or longer to blend flavors.

Makes 6 to 8 servings.

Caper Dressing

Mix 3 tablespoons red wine vinegar; 1 tablespoon *each* lemon juice and liquid from capers; 2 teaspoons Dijon mustard; ½ teaspoon *each* grated lemon rind, salt, and dried oregano; ⅛ teaspoon coarsely ground pepper; and 2 cloves garlic (minced or pressed). Using a fork or whisk, gradually beat in ⅔ cup olive oil or salad oil until well combined. Mix in 1 tablespoon drained capers. Makes about ¾ cup.

Savory Tortellini Salad

Stuffed pasta rings called *tortellini* make a colorful main dish salad to accompany with crusty hard rolls and a hearty red wine.

1 package (12 oz) frozen tortellini
3 tablespoons red wine vinegar
1 teaspoon *each* dried basil and Dijon mustard
¼ teaspoon salt
⅛ teaspoon coarsely ground pepper
1 clove garlic, minced or pressed
½ cup olive oil or salad oil
¼ cup finely chopped parsley
3 ounces (about ¾ cup) thin strips of dry salami
1 sweet red or green bell pepper, quartered, seeded, and cut into thin strips
2 tablespoons toasted pine nuts (optional)
2 tablespoons grated Parmesan cheese
   Butter or Boston lettuce

1. Cook tortellini according to package directions. Drain, rinse with cold water, and drain again. Set aside.
2. For dressing, in a large bowl mix vinegar, basil, mustard, salt, pepper, and garlic. Using a whisk or fork, gradually beat in oil until well combined.
3. Lightly mix in tortellini, parsley, salami, red pepper, pine nuts (if used), and cheese. Cover and refrigerate for 1 hour or longer to blend flavors. Serve on lettuce leaves.

Makes 4 to 6 servings.

Oriental Noodle Salad

The curly noodles in this salad, *chuka soba*, are the sort of precooked wheat flour noodles found in quick Oriental soup mixes. You should be able to find them in Oriental markets, packaged without the soup seasonings. The long strands of twisted spaghetti called *fusilli* can also be used, but require longer cooking (follow package directions for time). Sesame oil is the distinctive seasoning in this salad. If you would like to expand it to serve as a main dish, add shredded cooked chicken or finely diced ham.

4 ounces *chuka soba* noodles
   Boiling salted water
1 tablespoon Oriental sesame oil
2 tablespoons sesame seeds
2 cups (about 5 oz) fresh bean sprouts (see page 21)
   Boiling water
¼ pound small peeled, cooked shrimp
3 green onions, thinly sliced
1 stalk celery, thinly sliced on the diagonal
¼ pound mushrooms, thinly sliced
   Soy Dressing (recipe follows)

1. Add noodles to a large kettle of boiling salted water. When water returns to boiling and noodles come to top, cook until just tender, 2 to 3 minutes. (If another type of pasta is used, follow package directions.) Drain, rinse with cold water, and drain again. In a large bowl mix noodles with sesame oil; set aside.

Tortellini, stuffed pasta rings originally from Bologna, make a colorful crimson-and-white salad with salami and red pepper.

2. Stir sesame seeds in a small frying pan over medium heat until lightly browned (6 to 8 minutes); cool slightly.

3. Add bean sprouts to a large kettle of boiling water; when it returns to boiling, remove from heat, drain bean sprouts, rinse with cold water, and drain again; add to noodles. Cover and refrigerate for at least 1 hour.

4. To serve, lightly combine noodle mixture, sesame seeds, shrimp, onions, celery, mushrooms, and dressing.

Makes 4 to 6 servings.

Soy Dressing

In a small bowl mix ⅓ cup rice wine vinegar or white wine vinegar, 2 tablespoons *each* sugar and soy sauce, ¼ teaspoon *each* ground ginger and dry mustard, and a pinch cayenne pepper. Using a whisk or fork gradually mix in ¼ cup salad oil until well blended. Makes about ¾ cup.

🌿 Rice Salads

Rice Salad Niçoise

The colorful ingredients of the popular salad from the Côte d'Azur enliven this refreshing main dish rice salad.

2 cups water
1 teaspoon *each* olive oil or salad oil and salt
1 cup long grain rice
1 jar (6 oz) marinated artichoke hearts
1 can (2 oz) flat anchovy fillets, drained
1 green pepper, seeded and chopped
1 stalk celery, finely chopped
4 green onions, thinly sliced
¼ cup Niçoise olives or slivered ripe olives
½ cup chopped peeled cucumber
1 small tomato, seeded and chopped
1 can (6½ oz) chunk light tuna, drained and flaked

2 hard-cooked eggs, sliced
Garlic Vinaigrette Dressing (recipe follows)
Butter or Boston lettuce leaves
Tomato wedges, for garnish

1. In a 2-quart saucepan combine water, oil, and salt; bring to boiling. Gradually add rice. Cover, reduce heat, and simmer for 20 to 25 minutes, until rice is just tender. Lightly mix in artichoke hearts (with their marinade). Transfer to a large bowl, cover, and refrigerate until cool.

2. Reserving about 5 anchovy fillets for garnish, chop remaining anchovies. Add chopped anchovies to rice with green pepper, celery, green onions, olives, cucumber, chopped tomato, tuna, and hard-cooked eggs. Add dressing and mix lightly.

Cover and refrigerate for at least 2 hours to blend flavors.

3. Serve in a bowl lined with lettuce. Garnish with tomato wedges and reserved anchovies.

Makes 6 to 8 servings.

Garlic Vinaigrette Dressing

In a medium bowl mix 2 tablespoons red wine vinegar, 1½ teaspoons lemon juice, 2 teaspoons Dijon mustard, 1 clove garlic (minced or pressed), ¼ teaspoon salt, and a dash of coarsely ground black pepper. Using a whisk or fork, gradually blend in 2 tablespoons olive oil and ⅓ cup salad oil, mixing until well blended and slightly thickened. Stir in 1 tablespoon chopped parsley. Makes ½ cup.

Tuna and rice have never tasted better than in sprightly Rice Salad Niçoise.

A sweet-sour dressing and slivered red onions complement Rice and Bean Sprouts Salad.

Rice and Bean Sprouts Salad

Serve this wonderful tasting rice salad as you would a potato salad, with broiled or barbecued chicken. It is especially good when made with home-sprouted mung beans.

1 small red onion, slivered
2 cups mung bean sprouts (see page 21)
  Sweet-Sour Dressing (recipe follows)
1 cup water
¼ teaspoon *each* salt and Oriental sesame oil
½ cup long grain rice
¼ cup golden raisins
½ cup toasted slivered almonds
2 green onions, thinly sliced
½ cup chopped sweet red or green bell pepper
  Leaf lettuce

1. In a large bowl lightly mix red onion, bean sprouts, and dressing. Cover and refrigerate 1 to 2 hours.
2. Meanwhile, bring water to boiling in a medium saucepan with salt and oil. Mix in rice and raisins. Cover, reduce heat, and simmer for 20 to 25 minutes, until rice is just tender. Let cool to room temperature.
3. Add rice mixture to bean sprouts mixture with almonds, green onions, and red pepper. Mix lightly. Cover and refrigerate for at least 2 hours to blend flavors. Serve in a lettuce-lined bowl.

Makes 4 to 6 servings.

Sweet-Sour Dressing

In a medium bowl combine ⅓ cup rice wine vinegar, 2 teaspoons sugar, ½ teaspoon dried tarragon, 1 teaspoon salt, and a pinch of white pepper; stir until sugar dissolves. Using a whisk or fork, gradually beat in ⅓ cup salad oil until well combined. Makes about ⅔ cup.

Spiced Brown Rice Salad

The memorable flavors of this substantial brown rice salad make it a good accompaniment to baked ham, or as the centerpiece of a vegetable plate.

1½ cups water
1 teaspoon *each* salt and salad oil
¾ cup brown rice
¼ cup raisins
½ cup frozen peas
3 tablespoons white wine vinegar
½ teaspoon sugar
¼ teaspoon *each* ground cardamom and whole cloves
⅓ cup salad oil
  1-inch piece cinnamon stick
½ cup diced cucumber
⅓ cup coarsely chopped dry-roasted cashews
3 green onions, thinly sliced
¼ cup *each* mayonnaise and plain yogurt
  Red leaf lettuce

1. In a medium saucepan bring water to boiling with salt and the 1 teaspoon oil. Mix in rice and raisins.

Cover, reduce heat, and simmer for 40 to 45 minutes, until rice is just tender. Mix in peas and let cool to room temperature.
2. In a large bowl mix vinegar, sugar, cardamom, and cloves. Using a whisk or fork, gradually beat in the ⅓ cup salad oil until well combined. Lightly mix in cooled rice, cinnamon stick, cucumber, cashews, and green onions. Cover and refrigerate for about 2 hours to blend flavors.
3. Mix mayonnaise and yogurt until smooth. Fold into rice mixture. Serve in lettuce-lined bowl.

Makes 4 to 6 servings.

Pearl Rice Salad with Peas

Here is a pristine green-and-white salad to accompany grilled lamb or fish.

1½ cups water
1 chicken bouillon cube
1 teaspoon olive oil or salad oil
¾ cup pearl rice
1 cup frozen peas
5 green onions, thinly sliced
2 tablespoons chopped fresh parsley
  Lemon-Parmesan Dressing (recipe follows)

1. In a medium saucepan combine water, bouillon cube, and oil. Bring to boiling, stirring until bouillon cube dissolves. Gradually add rice. Cover, reduce heat, and simmer for 15 to 20 minutes, until rice is just tender. Lightly mix in peas. Transfer to a bowl and refrigerate until rice is cold.
2. Add green onions, parsley, and dressing; mix lightly. Let stand at room temperature for about 20 minutes before serving.

Makes 4 to 6 servings.

Lemon-Parmesan Dressing

In a small bowl mix 2 tablespoons lemon juice, 1 clove garlic (minced or pressed), ½ teaspoon grated lemon rind, ¼ teaspoon salt, a pinch white pepper, and 1 tablespoon grated Parmesan cheese. Using a whisk or fork, gradually beat in ⅓ cup olive oil or salad oil, mixing until thoroughly blended.
Makes about 6 tablespoons.

🦃 Bean Salads

Zesty Garbanzo Bean Salad

This colorful salad makes a fine contribution to a potluck picnic. If you would like to serve it as a main dish, add a can of drained, flaked tuna.

1 can (15½ oz) garbanzo beans (ceci beans or chick peas), drained
½ cup sliced pimiento-stuffed olives
½ cup chopped red onion
1 stalk celery, thinly sliced
¼ cup chopped fresh parsley
   Zesty Garlic Dressing (recipe follows)
   Romaine leaves
   Cherry tomatoes, for garnish

1. Lightly mix garbanzos, olives, onion, celery, and parsley. Mix in dressing, cover, and chill for 1 to 2 hours to blend flavors.
2. Serve in a bowl lined with romaine; garnish with tomatoes.

Makes 4 servings.

Zesty Garlic Dressing

In a small bowl mix 2 tablespoons red wine vinegar, 2 teaspoons Dijon mustard, ¼ teaspoon sugar, ⅛ teaspoon cayenne pepper, and 1 clove garlic (minced or pressed). Using a fork or whisk, gradually beat in ⅓ cup olive oil or salad oil until well combined. Makes about 6 tablespoons.

Red Bean Salad Ranchero

If you enjoy Mexican food, you will appreciate the lively seasonings in this colorful bean salad from the Southwest. It is good with barbecued spareribs or chili dogs.

1 cup dried small red beans, rinsed and drained
3 cups water
1 teaspoon salt
   Ranchero Dressing (recipe follows)
1 stalk celery, finely chopped
1 small onion, finely chopped
½ cup diced sharp Cheddar cheese (¼-in. cubes)

Barbecued spareribs make a hearty meal with Red Bean Salad Ranchero.

¼ cup *each* sliced ripe olives and chopped fresh parsley
1 small tomato, seeded and chopped
2 tablespoons green chile salsa
   Shredded iceberg lettuce
   Tortilla chips, for garnish

1. Bring beans and water to boiling. Boil briskly, uncovered, for 2 minutes. Cover, remove from heat, and let stand 1 hour.
2. To beans and liquid add salt. Bring to boiling, reduce heat, cover, and simmer until beans are tender (about 2 hours). Drain thoroughly.
3. To drained beans add about half of the dressing, cover, and refrigerate until cool.

4. Mix in celery, onion, cheese, olives, parsley, tomato, salsa, and remaining dressing. Cover and refrigerate for 1 to 3 hours to blend flavors.
5. Serve salad on individual plates lined with shredded lettuce; garnish with tortilla chips.

Makes 6 servings.

Ranchero Dressing

Mix ¼ cup red wine vinegar, 1 teaspoon *each* salt and sugar, ¼ teaspoon *each* dried oregano and ground cumin, a dash of cayenne pepper, and 1 clove garlic (minced or pressed). Beat in ½ cup olive oil or salad oil. Makes about ¾ cup.

Bistro Lentil Salad

Lentils cook quickly and make an unusual salad to accompany corned beef. This salad can be served either hot—mixed and served as soon as the lentils are cooked and drained—or cold.

1 cup dried lentils, rinsed and drained
½ teaspoon salt
1 bay leaf
¼ teaspoon dried thyme
1 carrot, shredded
3 cups water
1 small onion, finely chopped
¼ cup chopped fresh parsley
  Mustard Vinaigrette Dressing (recipe follows)
  Butter or Boston lettuce leaves

1. In a large saucepan combine lentils, salt, bay leaf, thyme, carrot, and water. Bring to boiling, cover, reduce heat, and boil gently until lentils are tender (25 to 30 minutes). Drain lentils thoroughly; discard bay leaf.
2. Mix lentils, onion, parsley, and dressing. If not served immediately, cover and refrigerate for 1 to 3 hours or overnight to blend flavors. Serve salad on lettuce leaves.

Makes 4 to 6 servings.

Mustard Vinaigrette Dressing

In a small bowl mix 3 tablespoons tarragon vinegar, 1 tablespoon coarse-grained Dijon mustard, 1 clove garlic (minced or pressed), and ¾ teaspoon salt. Using a whisk or fork, gradually beat in 2 tablespoons olive oil and ¼ cup salad oil until well blended and slightly thickened. Makes about ½ cup.

This abundant repast of barbecued beef rib bones, colorful pasta salad, and homemade apple pie is perfect for a spring evening. Garnish the ribs with cucumber sticks and celery fantans – both crisped in ice water for several hours in advance of the meal – and cherry tomatoes.

Barbecued Beef Bones

Creamy Ziti Salad

Celery and Cucumber Sticks

Hot Garlic French Bread

Brandied Apple Pie

Beer or Red Jug Wine

Coffee

🍃 Backyard Barbecue

A fine weekend evening in autumn or spring is a good time for this candlelit outdoor picnic supper. It features barbecued beef ribs and a colorful pasta salad.

Most of the meal can be prepared ahead: Marinate the meat, bake the pie for dessert, and mix the salad. Wrap the garlic bread in heavy foil and heat it on the grill as you barbecue the ribs.

Barbecued Beef Bones

This recipe uses the meaty bones cut from a standing rib roast of beef. Many supermarkets sell them separately. Allow about 1 pound—2 to 3 ribs, depending on size—for each person.

4 pounds (8 to 10) meaty beef rib bones
⅓ cup salad oil
¼ cup brandy
2 tablespoons *each* red wine vinegar and lemon juice
½ teaspoon salt
1 clove garlic, minced or pressed
¼ teaspoon *each* ground ginger and coarsely ground black pepper
2 tablespoons honey

1. Arrange bones in a shallow baking dish large enough to hold them in a single layer. Shake together or whirl in blender container oil, brandy, vinegar, lemon juice, salt, garlic, ginger, and pepper; pour over beef bones. Cover and refrigerate for several hours or overnight.

2. Remove bones from marinade, reserving marinade. Mix honey smoothly into marinade. To barbecue, place bones on grill about 5 inches above an even bed of glowing coals, bone sides down. When brown and crisp, turn and brush with marinade.

3. Continue cooking, basting occasionally, until browned on the meaty side (a total of 25 to 30 minutes).

Makes 4 servings.

Creamy Ziti Salad

8 ounces (about 2½ cups) ziti, mostaccioli, *or* penne
½ cup *each* mayonnaise and sour cream
1 tablespoon *each* prepared mustard and sweet pickle juice
¼ teaspoon seasoned pepper
1 medium green pepper, seeded and chopped
4 green onions, thinly sliced
⅓ cup chopped sweet pickles
3 hard-cooked eggs, chopped
¼ pound sliced mortadella, cut in thin strips
1 cup halved cherry tomatoes
Red leaf lettuce

1. Cook ziti according to package directions. Drain, rinse with cold water, and drain again. Set aside.

2. For dressing, in a large bowl mix mayonnaise, sour cream, mustard, pickle juice, and seasoned pepper until smooth.

3. To dressing add ziti, green pepper, onions, pickles, eggs, mortadella, and about ¾ cup of the tomatoes. Mix lightly to coat all ingredients with dressing. Cover and refrigerate for 1 hour or longer to blend flavors.

4. Serve in a lettuce-lined bowl, garnished with reserved ¼ cup cherry tomato halves.

Makes 4 to 6 servings.

Brandied Apple Pie

Pastry for a double-crust 9-inch pie
⅔ cup granulated sugar
⅓ cup light brown sugar
2 tablespoons quick-cooking tapioca
1 tablespoon cornstarch
½ teaspoon ground cinnamon
¼ teaspoon ground nutmeg
6 medium-size tart cooking apples, peeled, cored, and sliced
¼ cup brandy
1 tablespoon currant jelly
2 tablespoons butter or margarine

1. Roll out half of the pastry and place in a 9-inch pie pan.

2. Mix sugars, tapioca, cornstarch and spices; add to apple slices and gently stir to coat them with the mixture. Mound apples in pastry-lined pie pan.

3. In a small saucepan heat brandy and jelly until jelly melts; pour over apples. Dot with butter.

4. Roll out remaining pastry and cut into ¾-inch-wide lattice strips. Top apples with lattice crust; trim and flute edge.

5. Bake in a 375°F oven for 55 minutes to 1 hour, until pastry is golden brown and apples are tender and bubbly. Serve warm or cool.

Makes 1 pie: 6 to 8 servings.

FROMAGE

SAUCISS

Main Dish Salads

Practically any salad can serve as a meal. Your idea of a satisfying main dish is likely to depend on such variables as appetite, weather, and what is at hand. However, *all* the salads in this chapter are filling and nourishing enough to serve as the principal course of a meal.

Ingredients for these hearty salads are a delicatessen of favorite foods, including meat, sausages, chicken and turkey, cheese, and fish and seafood. These salads also make good use of small amounts of already cooked foods that may have accumulated in the refrigerator.

Both creamy and oil-and-vinegar dressings complement main dish salads. To reduce calories, try one of the recipes on page 91.

Garnish your full-meal salad artfully, present it with a flourish and a loaf of good bread—and lunch, supper, or dinner is served!

Cucumber-Lemon Beef Salad

Crisp cucumber slices and strips of pink-rare cold roast beef combine in this flavorful salad. Natural crispness, tender skin, and virtual seedlessness suit the long slender English hothouse cucumber (it may also be called a European, Holland, or Armenian cucumber) for this salad.

2   cups (about ¾ lb) thinly sliced lean, rare roast beef, cut in bite-size strips

Shop at your favorite delicatessen for the myriad of hearty ingredients in such dishes as the attractive Cobb Salad (shown at left, center; recipe on page 65) and Cucumber-Lemon Beef Salad (right).

½   seedless English cucumber, thinly sliced (1½ to 2 cups)
1   small red onion, thinly sliced and separated into rings
    Lemon Dressing (recipe follows)
2   tablespoons drained capers
¼   cup chopped fresh parsley
    Butter or Boston lettuce leaves
    Tomato and lemon wedges, for garnish

1. Combine beef, cucumber slices, and onion rings. Mix lightly with Lemon Dressing and capers; cover and refrigerate for 1 to 3 hours to blend flavors.

2. To serve, mix in parsley. Heap in shallow bowl or on platter lined with lettuce. Garnish with tomato and lemon wedges.

Makes 4 servings.

Lemon Dressing
In a small bowl combine 2 tablespoons lemon juice; 1 clove garlic (minced or pressed); ½ teaspoon *each* salt, sugar, grated lemon rind, and grated fresh ginger (or ¼ teaspoon ground ginger); and 1 teaspoon Dijon mustard. Using a whisk or fork, gradually beat in ¼ cup salad oil. Makes about ⅓ cup.

Bacon, chicken, and avocado encircle greens of Cobb Salad.

Deviled Roast Beef Salad

A favorite in German delicatessens, this colorful salad tastes good with a rye bread, sweet butter, and beer.

2 cups (about ¾ lb) thinly sliced lean, rare roast beef, cut in bite-size strips

½ cup thinly sliced celery

1 sweet red bell pepper, quartered, seeded, and cut in thin strips (or 1 large jar [4 oz] pimiento strips, drained)

¼ cup *each* sliced dill pickles, cut in thin strips; small pickled onions; and chopped fresh parsley
Sharp Mustard Dressing (recipe follows)
Red or green leaf lettuce
3 hard-cooked eggs, cut in wedges

1. Lightly mix beef, celery, red pepper, dill pickles, pickled onions, chopped parsley, and dressing.
2. Place beef mixture on lettuce in a serving bowl or on a platter. Garnish with egg wedges.
Makes 4 servings.

Sharp Mustard Dressing

In a small bowl combine 1 tablespoon red wine vinegar, ¼ teaspoon salt, ½ teaspoon sugar, 2 teaspoons Dijon mustard, and a dash white pepper. Using a whisk or fork, gradually beat in 1 tablespoon olive oil and 2 tablespoons salad oil until smooth. Makes about ¼ cup.

Favorite Chef's Salad

When you assemble it at home, quality ingredients make this popular restaurant salad even better. It includes ham or smoked tongue, tender strips of chicken or turkey, and aged Swiss cheese. The dressing is a creamy vinaigrette; you might also serve the salad with a blue cheese, Thousand Island, or clear oil-and-vinegar dressing. Line the serving bowl with some of the outside romaine or iceberg lettuce leaves.

6 cups *each* torn romaine and iceberg lettuce

½ cup thinly sliced radishes

4 green onions, thinly sliced
Chef's Dressing (recipe follows)

1 cup julienne chicken *or* turkey

1 cup julienne ham *or* smoked tongue

¼ pound julienne Swiss cheese (about 1 cup)

2 tomatoes, each cut into 6 wedges

3 hard-cooked eggs, each cut into 4 wedges
Radish roses, for garnish

1. In a large bowl lightly mix romaine, iceberg lettuce, sliced radishes, green onions, and half of the dressing.
2. Mix chicken, ham, and cheese; scatter over top of salad. Arrange tomato and egg wedges around edge. Garnish with radish roses.
3. Pour remaining dressing over center of salad, or place in a bowl or pitcher and bring to the table.
Makes 4 servings.

Chef's Dressing

In a medium bowl mix 1 egg yolk, 3 tablespoon red wine vinegar, 1 tablespoon Dijon mustard, 1 clove garlic (minced or pressed), 1 teaspoon prepared horseradish, ½ teaspoon salt, and ⅛ teaspoon paprika until well combined. Using a whisk or fork, gradually beat in ¼ cup olive oil and ½ cup salad oil until dressing is slightly thickened and creamy. Mix in 1 tablespoon chopped fresh parsley.
Makes about 1 cup.

Garlic Sausage Salad

Vegetable relishes such as carrot sticks, cucumber slices, and radishes are a perfect accompaniment to this salad.

1 pound plump garlic sausages (knockwurst)
  Boiling water
  Creamy Mustard and Shallot Dressing (recipe follows)
  Butter or Boston lettuce leaves
  Chopped fresh parsley, for garnish
  Ripe olives
1 hard-cooked egg, cut in wedges

1. Pierce each sausage in several places with a fork. Place in a deep frying pan large enough to hold sausages in a single layer and cover with boiling water. Cook, covered, over low heat for 15 minutes. (Do not allow water to boil; it should remain just under the boiling point.) Drain sausages.
2. Remove sausage casings, slice meat thinly, and place slices in a bowl.
3. Mix lightly with dressing. (If made ahead, cover and refrigerate up to 3 hours until ready to serve.)
4. Serve in a shallow bowl lined with lettuce. Sprinkle with parsley and garnish with olives and egg wedges.

Makes 4 servings.

Creamy Mustard and Shallot Dressing

In a medium bowl mix 1 egg yolk, 1 tablespoon white wine vinegar, 1½ teaspoons Dijon mustard, a dash of cayenne pepper, and 1 shallot (finely chopped). Using a fork or whisk, gradually beat in ⅓ cup salad oil until dressing is thick and creamy. Makes about ½ cup.

Technique Tips—*Garnishes*

Tomatoes. *For zigzag-cut tomatoes, make wedge-shaped cuts as shown above.*

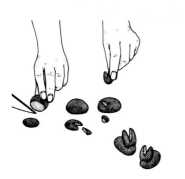

Olives. *Cut a slice from the bottom of an unpitted olive; cut a wedge from the slice. Cut another wedge from the olive, and insert the "rabbit ears."*

Carrots. *To make carrot curls, cut thin slices from a fat carrot with a vegetable peeler; roll each; hold with a pick; place in ice water.*

Radishes. *For radish roses, nip off root ends and most of leaves; then carefully cut a slice in each side. Crisp in ice water.*

Cobb Salad

This salad of southern California origin is a club sandwich in a salad bowl. Chicken, avocado, blue cheese, and crisp bacon are highlighted.

4 cups *each* torn butter or Boston lettuce and romaine
1 cup watercress sprigs (discard coarse stems)
1 large tomato, seeded and chopped
  Blue Cheese Vinaigrette Dressing (recipe follows)
2 hard-cooked eggs, whites and yolks shredded separately
6 slices bacon, crisply cooked, drained, and crumbled
1 medium avocado, peeled, seeded, and diced
2 whole chicken breasts (4 halves, about 2 lbs), cooked (see page 75) and cut into bite-size pieces

1. In a large bowl lightly mix lettuces, watercress, and tomato. Mix gently with about a third of the dressing.
2. Arrange remaining ingredients on lettuce mixture with egg yolks in center, surrounded by rings of egg whites, bacon, avocado, and chicken.
3. Serve salad onto individual plates; accompany with remaining dressing in a bowl or pitcher to add to each serving to taste.

Makes 4 servings.

Blue Cheese Vinaigrette Dressing

In a medium bowl mix 3 tablespoons tarragon wine vinegar, 2 tablespoons lemon juice, 1 tablespoon Dijon mustard, and 1 teaspoon salt. Using a whisk or fork gradually beat in ¼ cup olive oil and ⅓ cup salad oil until slightly thickened and well combined. Mix in ¼ cup crumbled blue-veined cheese. Makes about 1 cup.

Hot Chicken-Walnut Salad

Hot chicken and cold lettuce contrast elegantly in a salad that brings together Chinese stir-fry technique and French flavors. The heat of the quickly cooked chicken-and-walnut mixture wilts the greens slightly.

4   cups *each* torn romaine and chicory
1   cup cherry tomato halves
2   whole chicken breasts (4 halves, about 2 lbs), boned and skinned
    Salt and white pepper
1   tablespoon *each* walnut oil and salad oil
4   green onions, thinly sliced
1   clove garlic, minced or pressed
¼   cup coarsely chopped walnuts
1   tablespoon tarragon wine vinegar
    Walnut Oil Dressing (recipe follows)

1. Lightly mix romaine, chicory, and cherry tomatoes; cover and refrigerate if done ahead.
2. Pound chicken breasts between pieces of waxed paper, using flat side of a meat mallet, to a thickness of about ¼ inch. Cut into bite-size strips about ½ inch wide; sprinkle with salt and pepper.
3. In mixture of heated oils in a large frying pan lightly brown half the chicken, stirring and turning over medium-high heat until cooked through (about 3 minutes); remove from pan. Add remaining chicken and cook it as above. Return all the chicken to the pan and mix in green onions, garlic, and walnuts. Cook, stirring, until onions are limp (about 2 minutes). Stir in vinegar; remove from heat.
4. Place greens on 4 plates. Spoon hot chicken mixture over greens, dividing it evenly. Serve with dressing to add to each serving to taste.

Makes 4 servings.

Walnut Oil Dressing

In a medium bowl mix 2 tablespoons tarragon wine vinegar, 1 teaspoon lemon juice, 2 teaspoons Dijon mustard, ¼ teaspoon salt, and ⅛ teaspoon white pepper. Using a whisk or fork, gradually beat in 3 tablespoons walnut oil and ⅓ cup salad oil until well blended and thickened. Makes ⅔ cup.

Palace Court Salad

In recognition of its San Francisco background (it was created at the Palace Hotel and is still a standard in the Garden Court dining room), sourdough French bread and a California white wine seem to belong with this salad. Usually a choice of fillings — tuna, shrimp, chicken, or crab — is offered. This version departs from tradition by using a mixture of chicken and shrimp.

1   can (14 oz) artichoke bottoms, drained
    Thousand Island Dressing (recipe follows)
    Green leaf lettuce
2   tomatoes, sliced
3   cups diced cooked chicken
¼   pound small peeled, cooked shrimp
1   hard-cooked egg, shredded
    Ripe olives, for garnish

1. Fill each artichoke bottom with 1 tablespoon of the dressing and place it on a lettuce-lined plate. Surround with tomato slices.
2. Lightly mix chicken, shrimp, and ½ cup of the dressing; mound a sixth of the mixture on each artichoke bottom.
3. Drizzle a generous spoonful of the remaining dressing over each salad. Sprinkle shredded egg over each serving. Garnish with olives. Serve remaining dressing in a bowl to add at the table.

Makes 6 servings.

Thousand Island Dressing

Mix until smooth ½ cup *each* mayonnaise and sour cream, ¼ cup chili sauce, 1 tablespoon lemon juice, and a pinch of cayenne pepper. Mix in 1 hard-cooked egg (shredded), ⅓ cup finely chopped stuffed olives, and ¼ cup finely chopped sweet pickles. Cover and refrigerate for 1 to 3 hours to blend flavors. Makes about 1¾ cups.

During the brief season of fresh apricots, enjoy this fruited chicken salad.

Pineapple, Ham, and Chicken Wedges

Fruit shells make dramatic containers for main dish salads accented with fresh fruit. Here is a spectacular example—slivered chicken and ham mounded in fresh pineapple wedges.

1   medium pineapple (3 to 4 lbs)
2   cups diced or shredded cooked chicken
1   cup slivered baked ham
2   green onions, thinly sliced
½   cup sour cream
¼   cup mayonnaise
1   teaspoon Dijon mustard
⅛   teaspoon ground ginger

1. Cut pineapple into quarters, lengthwise, cutting through and keeping crown of leaves attached. Cut out and discard core. Remove fruit from each quarter, reserving shells. Cut half of the fruit into bite-size pieces. (Reserve remainder for other uses.)
2. To pineapple add chicken, ham, and green onions.
3. For dressing, mix sour cream, mayonnaise, mustard, and ginger. Mix lightly with pineapple mixture.
4. Mound salad in reserved shells. Serve garnished, if you wish, with additional sliced green onion.

Makes 4 servings.

   Note: If salad mixture is made ahead, wait to add pineapple until just before serving.

Serve elegant Hot Chicken-Walnut Salad either as a light supper or a luncheon main dish.

Chicken Salad with Apricots and Avocados

The sweet-tartness of apricots is an appealing foil for chicken and avocado. On a hot summer evening you will enjoy this salad with a chilled dry rosé or a *blanc de noir* (one of the faintly blushing "white" wines made from purple grapes).

3   cups cubed cooked chicken
1½ cups slivered apricots (unpeeled, pitted)
⅓   cup thinly sliced celery
¼   cup thinly sliced green onions
⅓   cup *each* mayonnaise and sour cream
1   tablespoon dry vermouth
½   teaspoon grated lemon rind
⅛   teaspoon ground nutmeg
1   avocado, peeled, seeded, and sliced
1   tablespoon lime *or* lemon juice
    Butter or Boston lettuce leaves
¼   cup toasted sliced almonds

1. Lightly mix chicken, apricots, celery, and green onions.
2. For dressing, in a small bowl mix mayonnaise, sour cream, vermouth, lemon rind, and nutmeg until smooth. Combine with chicken mixture, mixing lightly until well coated. Cover and refrigerate for 1 to 3 hours to blend flavors.
3. Brush avocado slices well on all sides with lime juice. Line 4 plates with lettuce leaves; divide chicken mixture onto the plates. Garnish each serving with a fourth of the avocado slices. Sprinkle with almonds.

Makes 4 servings

Hawaiian Chicken Salad

Use your artistic ability to arrange this chicken and fruit salad appealingly. Hot biscuits, preserves, and iced tea complete this spring lunch.

3   whole chicken breasts (6 halves, about 3 lbs), prepared through step 2 (see page 75) and chilled
    Shredded iceberg lettuce
1   small pineapple (about 2 lbs), peeled, cored, and cut in long, thin wedges
2   ripe avocados, peeled, seeded, and sliced
2   bananas, peeled and cut diagonally into ½-inch slices
2   kiwi fruit, peeled and sliced (optional)
    Chutney Dressing (recipe follows)
¼   cup chopped macadamia nuts
    Thinly sliced green onions and whole strawberries, for garnish

1. Cut chicken breasts in crosswise strips about ½ inch wide. Divide chicken into 4 portions and arrange each on lettuce in the center of a large chilled individual plate.
2. Surround with pineapple wedges, avocado and banana slices, and kiwi fruit (if used). Spoon a little dressing over the chicken and fruits. Sprinkle with nuts and green onions. Garnish with strawberries.
3. Serve immediately with remaining dressing in a small bowl to add at the table.

Makes 4 servings.

Chutney Dressing

In a medium bowl, mix until smooth ⅓ cup *each* mayonnaise and sour cream, ¼ cup Major Grey—type chutney (snip with kitchen scissors to dice fruit finely), ¼ teaspoon *each* salt and curry powder, a dash of Tabasco sauce, and 1 tablespoon white wine vinegar. Makes about ¾ cup.

Hot Swiss Turkey Salad

Here is a hot salad, which might seem to be a contradiction in terms. However, it is baked so briefly that all the vegetables retain their crispness. Add spiced peaches or cranberry sauce for flavor contrast.

¼ cup *each* mayonnaise and
  sour cream
1 tablespoon dry sherry
2 teaspoons Dijon mustard
¼ teaspoon dried tarragon
3 cups diced or shredded cooked
  turkey

1 stalk celery, finely chopped
4 green onions, thinly sliced
1 cup shredded Swiss cheese
½ cup slivered almonds

1. For dressing, mix mayonnaise, sour cream, sherry, mustard, and tarragon until smooth.
2. Lightly combine dressing, turkey, celery, green onions, and cheese. Divide the turkey mixture into 4 to 6 individual greased shallow baking dishes. Top with almonds. (At this point salads can be covered and refrigerated for several hours.)
3. Bake, uncovered, in a 400°F oven for 15 to 20 minutes (20 to 25 minutes if refrigerated) until salads are bubbly and almonds lightly browned.

Makes 4 to 6 servings.

Marinated Chicken Breasts and Vegetable Salad

This gingery salad makes a handsome presentation on a deep platter, when chicken breasts alternate with clusters of marinated broccoli and carrots.

3 whole chicken breasts (6 halves, about 3 lbs), prepared through step 2 (see page 75)
⅓ cup tarragon vinegar
1 tablespoon Dijon mustard
2 shallots, finely chopped
½ teaspoon ground ginger
¾ teaspoon salt
⅓ cup olive oil
⅔ cup salad oil
2 cups broccoli flowerets
1 cup thinly sliced carrots
  Red leaf lettuce
  Chopped parsley, for garnish

1. Place chicken breasts in a single layer in a shallow dish.
2. In a medium bowl mix vinegar, mustard, shallots, ginger, and salt. Using a whisk or fork, gradually beat in oils until slightly thickened and well combined. Drizzle about half of the dressing over chicken breasts; cover chicken and remaining dressing and refrigerate at least 2 hours, until ready to serve.
3. Shortly before serving arrange broccoli and carrots on a rack over boiling water; steam until tender-crisp (5 to 6 minutes). Drain, rinse with cold water, and drain again. Mix vegetables lightly with remaining dressing.
4. Arrange marinated chicken breasts and vegetables with dressing on a lettuce-lined plate. Sprinkle with parsley.

Makes 6 servings.

Make an informal supper of chicken breasts and marinated vegetables.

Italian Antipasto Salad Bowl

Use any two of the salad greens suggested for this Italian-accented chef's salad. Appropriate accompaniments include hot garlic bread, a red jug wine, and fresh peaches or nectarines for dessert.

1   jar (6 oz) marinated artichoke hearts
1   small can (8¾ oz) garbanzo beans, drained
1   small can (8¾ oz) red kidney beans, drained
1   can (6½ oz) chunk light tuna, drained and flaked
½   sweet red onion, thinly sliced and separated into rings
2   to 3 tablespoons bottled Italian-style salad dressing
½   cup thinly sliced celery
6   cups torn salad greens, such as romaine, chicory, red leaf, or iceberg lettuce
1   can (2 oz) flat anchovy fillets, drained (optional)
3   ounces thinly sliced dry salami, cut in thin strips
2   ounces fontina cheese, cut in ¼-inch cubes (about ½ cup)
     Pickled sweet red and green peppers, for garnish

1. Mix artichoke hearts and their marinade with garbanzo and kidney beans, tuna, onion, and 2 tablespoons of the bottled dressing. Cover and refrigerate for 1 hour or longer to blend flavors.
2. In a large salad bowl lightly combine the marinated mixture with celery and and salad greens. If needed, mix in a little more bottled dressing.
3. Over the top arrange anchovies (if used), salami, and cheese. Garnish with red and green peppers. Serve at once.

Makes 4 servings.

New Mexico Chalupa-Style Salad

In New Mexico a *chalupa* (cha-*loo*-pah) is a little boat made from tortilla dough. It is filled with a cargo of savory tidbits. In this adaptation, all the delicious fillings are present, but tortilla chips substitute for the *chalupa*.

1   cup dried pinto or pink beans
3   cups water
1   medium onion, chopped
1   small dried red pepper, crushed
1   teaspoon salt
1   tablespoon lemon juice
2   tablespoons olive oil or salad oil
3   cups shredded cooked chicken *or* turkey
     Red leaf lettuce
     New Mexico Guacamole (recipe follows)
     Sour cream, for garnish
1   cup shredded Cheddar cheese
     Tortilla chips and radish roses, for garnish
     Green chile salsa

1. Rinse and drain beans. Bring beans and water to boiling in a 2-quart saucepan; boil briskly for 2 minutes; then remove from heat and let stand, covered, for 1 hour. Add onion, red pepper, and ½ teaspoon of the salt. Bring to boiling, cover, reduce heat, and simmer, stirring occasionally, until beans are tender and liquid is absorbed (about 2½ hours). Let stand until lukewarm.
2. Mix lemon juice, olive oil, and remaining ½ teaspoon salt; mix lightly with chicken. Line each of 4 plates generously with red leaf lettuce. Spread a fourth of the beans in center of each plate; cover each portion with ¾ cup of the chicken mixture, a fourth of the guacamole, a dollop of sour cream, and ¼ cup cheese.
3. Garnish each serving generously with tortilla chips, add a few radish roses, and offer salsa to add to taste.

Makes 4 servings.

New Mexico Guacamole

Halve, seed, and peel 2 soft-ripe avocados. Mash with 1 tablespoon lime juice until mixture is soft but still chunky. Lightly mix in ¼ cup finely chopped red onion, 1 small tomato (seeded and chopped), 2 tablespoons chopped fresh cilantro *or* parsley, ¼ teaspoon salt, and a dash *each* Tabasco sauce and seasoned pepper. Makes about 2 cups.

Chalupa-Style Salad layers pink beans, marinated chicken, guacamole, sour cream, and cheese, enwreathed by crisp corn chips.

Chicken Salad in Cantaloupe Bowls

The intense, bittersweet flavor of kumquats strikes an unusual note in this chicken salad combination. Be sure the cantaloupe is perfectly ripe for maximum flavor.

3   cups cubed cooked chicken
½   cup thinly sliced celery
2   green onions, thinly sliced
3   preserved kumquats, thinly sliced and seeds removed
⅓   cup *each* mayonnaise and sour cream
2   tablespoons orange-flavored liqueur
1   teaspoon Dijon mustard
½   teaspoon salt
2   medium cantaloupes, halved and seeded
    Lettuce leaves
    Strawberries, for garnish

1. Mix chicken, celery, green onions, and kumquats in a large bowl.
2. In a medium bowl, smoothly mix mayonnaise, sour cream, orange liqueur, mustard, and salt; blend lightly with chicken mixture. If you wish, cover and refrigerate for ½ to 3 hours to blend flavors.
3. Mound chicken mixture in cantaloupe halves. Serve on lettuce leaves, garnished with strawberries.
Makes 4 servings.

Poached Salmon with Mint Dressing

Mint is a refreshing complement to cold salmon. You might cook green beans tender-crisp, cool, and serve them on the same plate with some of the dressing for the fish.

3   green onions, thinly sliced
2   sprigs fresh parsley
6   whole white or black peppercorns
¼   teaspoon fennel seeds, slightly crushed
3   tablespoons tarragon wine vinegar
1   teaspoon salt
½   cup dry white wine
1   quart water

At the center of this Niçoise salad is a poached fish steak, garnished with vegetables.

4   salmon steaks (1½ to 2 lbs), about ¾ inch thick
    Mint Dressing (recipe follows)
    Butter or Boston lettuce leaves
    Lemon wedges, tomato halves, and mint sprigs, for garnish

1. In a large deep frying pan combine onions, parsley, peppercorns, fennel seeds, vinegar, salt, wine, and water. Bring to boiling, cover, reduce heat, and simmer for 20 minutes.
2. Lower salmon steaks into simmering liquid, cover, reduce heat, and cook just until salmon begins to separate into flakes when tested with a fork (8 to 10 minutes).
3. Remove salmon steaks with a slotted spatula and place in a shallow dish; drizzle with about half of the dressing. Cover and refrigerate until ready to serve (at least 2 hours).
4. Serve on lettuce leaves, garnished with lemon wedges and tomato halves topped with mint sprigs. Serve with remaining dressing to add to taste.
Makes 4 servings.

Mint Dressing

In a medium bowl mix ¼ cup lemon juice, 2 tablespoons tarragon wine vinegar, 2 shallots (finely chopped), 2 teaspoons Dijon mustard, 2 tablespoons chopped fresh mint leaves, ½ teaspoon salt, and ⅛ teaspoon white pepper. Using a whisk or fork, gradually beat in ¼ cup olive oil and ½ cup salad oil. Makes about 1 cup.

Poached Fish Salad Niçoise

Large steaks from your choice of several varieties of firm, white-fleshed fish are the centerpiece of this striking arrangement of raw and cooked vegetables enhanced by a garlic-flavored oil-and-vinegar dressing.

Poaching Liquid (recipe follows)
2 large fish steaks (about 2 lbs), such as halibut, swordfish, sea bass, or shark
Tarragon Dressing (recipe follows)
2 medium boiling potatoes (about 1 lb)
Salted water
1 pound whole green beans
Green leaf lettuce
4 long, thin strips carrot (cut with a potato peeler)
2 tomatoes, cut into wedges
3 hard-cooked eggs, cut into wedges
½ seedless English cucumber, thinly sliced
1 head Belgian endive, separated into leaves
1 can (2 oz) whole anchovy fillets
1 small red onion, thinly sliced and separated into rings
Niçoise or other black olives
Fresh tarragon or parsley sprigs, for garnish

1. Bring Poaching Liquid to a simmer in a large deep frying pan that will hold fish steaks in a single layer. Lower fish into simmering liquid, cover, reduce heat, and cook just until fish separates into flakes when tested with a fork (8 to 10 minutes). Remove bones and skin from fish and discard; cut each steak in half and place in a shallow dish. Drizzle with ¼ cup of the dressing. Cover and refrigerate until ready to serve (at least 2 hours).
2. Cook potatoes (scrubbed, unpeeled) in boiling salted water until tender (25 to 35 minutes). While warm, slice crosswise about ⅛ inch thick, place in a shallow dish, and drizzle with ¼ cup of the dressing. Cover and refrigerate at least 2 hours.
3. Shortly before serving, cook green beans, uncovered, in a large quantity of boiling salted water until tender-crisp (about 8 minutes). Drain, rinse with cold water, and drain again.
4. To serve, cover each of 4 plates with lettuce. Place a fish steak half in center. Arrange potato slices at side. Add a neat group of beans, encircling the center of each bundle with a carrot strip. Arrange tomatoes, eggs, cucumber, and endive leaves artfully on plates. Place an anchovy fillet inside each endive leaf. Scatter onion rings over fish and potatoes. Garnish each plate with olives and a sprig of tarragon.

Makes 4 servings.

Poaching Liquid

In a large deep frying pan combine 1 medium onion (sliced), 2 sprigs fresh parsley, 6 whole black peppercorns, 2 whole allspice, 3 tablespoons tarragon wine vinegar, 1 bay leaf, 1 teaspoon salt, ½ cup dry white wine, and 1 quart water. Bring to boiling, cover, reduce heat, and simmer for 20 minutes. After poaching fish, strain liquid and freeze for another use.

Tarragon Dressing

In a medium bowl mix ⅓ cup tarragon wine vinegar, 1 large clove garlic (minced or pressed), 2 tablespoons Dijon mustard, ½ teaspoon *each* salt and sugar, and ⅛ teaspoon *each* dried thyme and white pepper. Using a whisk or fork, gradually beat in ½ cup *each* olive oil and salad oil until slightly thickened and well combined. Makes about 1½ cups.

Artichoke and King Crab Plate

Here is a spectacular eat-with-your-fingers combination: fresh artichokes, king crab legs, and homemade lemon mayonnaise. Serve with sourdough French bread. Try it using cracked Dungeness crab also.

3 quarts water
¼ cup cider vinegar
1 bay leaf
1 teaspoon salt
¼ teaspoon *each* whole black peppercorns and dried thyme
1 tablespoon olive oil or salad oil
4 medium to large artichokes
Green leaf lettuce
4 cooked Alaska king crab legs (about 3 lbs), in shell, thawed if frozen
Cherry tomatoes, for garnish
Mustard-Lemon Mayonnaise (recipe follows)

1. In a 5-quart (or larger) kettle combine water, vinegar, bay leaf, salt, peppercorns, thyme, and olive oil. Bring to boiling.
2. Meanwhile, cut off the thorny end of each artichoke and, using kitchen scissors, cut thorns from tips of remaining leaves. Remove and discard small leaves at base; cut off stem. Place artichokes in boiling water and boil gently, covered, until tender when stem end is pierced with a fork (30 to 40 minutes). Drain and cool to room temperature, or refrigerate until ready to serve.
3. Serve artichokes on plates lined with lettuce, accompanied by crab legs and garnished with tomatoes. Serve a small bowl of mayonnaise at each place as a dipping sauce for artichoke leaves and crab.

Makes 4 servings.

Mustard-Lemon Mayonnaise

In a blender or food processor combine 1 egg, 2 teaspoons Dijon mustard, 2 tablespoons lemon juice, 1 teaspoon grated lemon peel, 1 clove garlic (minced or pressed), ¼ teaspoon salt, and a pinch cayenne pepper. Cover and begin to whirl or process; *immediately* begin adding, in a slow, steady stream, ¼ cup olive oil and ¾ cup salad oil until all the oil is added and mayonnaise is thick and smooth. Makes about 1¼ cups.

Tomatoes Stuffed with Peas and Shrimp

For a light meal when ripe tomatoes are at their peak, choose this combination.

¼ cup *each* mayonnaise and sour cream
1 teaspoon *each* tarragon wine vinegar and Dijon mustard
½ teaspoon *each* salt and dried dill weed
1 package (10 oz) frozen peas
½ pound small peeled, cooked shrimp
2 hard-cooked eggs, chopped
¼ cup sweet pickle relish
1 stalk celery, finely chopped
4 to 6 medium tomatoes
Butter or Boston lettuce

1. In a medium bowl mix mayonnaise, sour cream, vinegar, mustard, salt, and dill weed until smooth.
2. Cook peas according to package directions until just tender; drain well, rinse with cold water, and drain again.
3. To mayonnaise mixture add peas, shrimp, eggs, pickle relish, and celery. Mix lightly to coat. Cover and refrigerate for 1 to 3 hours to blend flavors.
4. To serve, core tomatoes (peel, if you wish). Separate each into 6 wedges, cutting almost to, *but not through,* bottom. Spread sections slightly. Lightly salt cut surfaces. Place tomatoes on lettuce.
5. Divide shrimp mixture evenly among the 4 to 6 tomatoes, filling them attractively.

Makes 4 to 6 servings.

Tiny shrimp fill papaya boats (above) and wedge-cut stuffed tomatoes (below).

Papaya Boats with Sesame Shrimp

Buttery-sweet papaya combines deliciously with tiny shrimp in a sesame-and-citrus dressing. You might accompany this full-meal salad with iced tea and warm Orange Sugar Biscuits (page 49).

2   tablespoons sesame seeds

2   tablespoons lime *or* lemon juice

½   teaspoon grated lime *or* lemon rind

½   teaspoon dry mustard

⅛   teaspoon *each* salt and ground cumin
    Pinch *each* ground coriander and cayenne pepper

⅓   cup salad oil

1   pound small peeled, cooked shrimp

½   cup finely chopped celery

2   green onions, thinly sliced

2   ripe papayas
    Shredded iceberg lettuce
    Sour cream
    Lime and orange wedges

1. Stir sesame seeds in a small frying pan over medium heat until lightly browned (6 to 8 minutes); cool slightly.

2. In a medium bowl mix lime juice, lime rind, mustard, salt, cumin, coriander, and cayenne. Gradually beat in salad oil, using a fork or whisk, until well combined. Stir in 4 teaspoons of the sesame seeds, reserving remainder for garnish. Lightly mix in shrimp, celery, and green onions. Cover and refrigerate for 1 to 2 hours to blend flavors.

3. Peel papayas. Cut in half and scoop out seeds. Place each half on a salad plate lined with shredded lettuce. Fill each half with a fourth of the shrimp mixture. Top each with a dollop of sour cream and sprinkle with reserved sesame seeds. Garnish with lime and orange wedges.

Makes 4 servings.

Crab Louis, made with fresh Dungeness crab and a creamy dressing, is a Western classic with chilled Chardonnay and sliced sourdough French bread.

Crab Louis

The dressing for this classic salad, similar to a Thousand Island dressing, also goes well with cold shrimp, lobster, or poached fish.

4   whole green outer iceberg-lettuce leaves

6   cups shredded iceberg lettuce

1   pound cooked crabmeat (or ½ lb *each* small peeled, cooked shrimp and crabmeat)
    Louis Dressing (recipe follows)

2   medium tomatoes, cut in wedges

2   hard-cooked eggs, cut in wedges
    Capers and ripe olives, for garnish

1. On each of 4 plates or in broad, shallow bowls, place a whole lettuce leaf. Fill with shredded lettuce.

2. Flake crabmeat, reserving whole leg pieces. Divide crabmeat evenly among the 4 servings, garnishing with leg pieces. Spoon about half of the dressing over crab.

3. Garnish each serving with tomatoes, egg wedges, capers, and olives. Serve additional dressing in a bowl to add to each serving to taste.

Makes 4 servings.

Louis Dressing

Mix until smooth ½ cup *each* mayonnaise and sour cream, ¼ cup chili sauce, 1 tablespoon lemon juice, and a pinch of cayenne pepper. Mix in ⅓ cup finely chopped green pepper and 2 green onions (thinly sliced). Cover and refrigerate for 1 to 3 hours to blend flavors. Makes about 1½ cups.

Green Goddess Shrimp Salad

Anchovies give the creamy green dressing for this romaine, mushroom, and shrimp salad a tangy saltiness.

1 tablespoon *each* lemon juice and tarragon vinegar
1 clove garlic, minced or pressed
2 tablespoons finely chopped canned anchovy fillets
3 green onions, sliced
½ cup lightly packed fresh parsley leaves
¼ cup sour cream
⅛ teaspoon white pepper
½ cup mayonnaise
8 cups torn romaine
¼ pound mushrooms, sliced
1 pound shrimp, cooked, shelled, and deveined (see page 75)

1. In blender or food processor combine lemon juice, vinegar, garlic, anchovies, green onions, and parsley; whirl or process until parsley is finely chopped. Add sour cream and pepper and whirl or process until blended. Transfer dressing to a bowl and smoothly mix in mayonnaise. (If made ahead, cover and refrigerate.)
2. Mix romaine, mushrooms, and about half of the dressing. Lightly mix in shrimp, reserving a few for garnish.
3. Serve salad garnished with reserved shrimp and accompanied by remaining dressing in a bowl, to add to taste.

Makes 4 servings.

Cheese Puffs with Mushroom Salad

Adding cheese to cream puff dough gives a crusty sheen and savory flavor to the product. (The French call the bread that results from this addition *gougère*.) Remove the tops from the cheese puffs while they are hot, fill with a fresh mushroom salad, and you have a glorious main dish for brunch or lunch.

Cheese Puffs (recipe follows)
2 tablespoons red wine vinegar
2 teaspoons Dijon mustard
½ teaspoon salt

¼ teaspoon white pepper
⅛ teaspoon dried oregano
2 tablespoons olive oil
¼ cup salad oil
¾ pound mushrooms, thinly sliced
2 tablespoons finely chopped fresh parsley
¼ cup slivered red onion
½ cup sliced cucumber half-moons (see note)

1. While Cheese Puffs bake, prepare salad dressing. In a small bowl mix vinegar, mustard, salt, pepper, and oregano. Using a whisk or fork, gradually beat in olive oil and salad oil until dressing is well combined and slightly thickened.
2. In a bowl combine mushrooms, parsley, onion, and cucumber. Mix lightly with dressing just before serving.
3. Cut a slice from top of each Cheese Puff. Place a fourth of the mushroom mixture in each of the 4 puffs; replace tops. Serve at once.

Makes 4 servings.

Cheese Puffs

Heat 1 cup milk and ¼ cup butter or margarine in a medium saucepan; add ½ teaspoon salt and a dash *each* nutmeg and white pepper. Bring to a full boil; add 1 cup all-purpose flour all at once, stirring over medium heat until mixture leaves sides of pan and forms a ball (about 2 minutes). Remove pan from heat. Beat in 4 eggs, one at a time, beating

A freshly baked, hot cheese puff makes an unusual salad bowl for marinated mushroom salad.

after each addition until mixture is smooth and glossy. Stir in ½ cup shredded Cheddar cheese.

Drop mixture in 4 equal mounds, about 2 inches apart, on a greased baking sheet. Mix ¼ cup *each* shredded Cheddar and Parmesan cheeses; sprinkle evenly over cheese puffs. Bake in a preheated 375°F oven until puffs are well browned and crisp (40 to 45 minutes). Serve hot. Makes 4 large puffs.

Note: To prepare cucumber, peel alternate ½-inch strips from skin; cut cucumber in half lengthwise. Scoop out and discard seeds; then cut into thin half-moon-shaped slices.

Anchovy, Cream Cheese, and Tomato Sandwiches

A homemade bread, such as the loaf made with sprouted wheat on page 49, is the perfect foundation for this salad in a sandwich.

1 package (3 oz) cream cheese, softened
2 tablespoons snipped chives *or* thinly sliced green onions
⅛ teaspoon seasoned pepper
4 thick slices Sprouted Wheat Berry Bread (see page 49) or other whole-grain bread
  Mayonnaise
1 can (2 oz) flat anchovy fillets, drained
2 slices tomato
  Green leaf lettuce
2 small wedges watermelon, for garnish

1. Mix cream cheese, chives, and pepper.
2. Spread each of 2 slices bread with half of the cream cheese mixture; spread remaining 2 slices with mayonnaise. Top each portion of cream cheese with half the anchovy fillets. Cover each with a tomato slice and a lettuce leaf. Top sandwiches with mayonnaise-spread bread slices, mayonnaise sides down.
3. Cut each sandwich in half; garnish each plate with a piece of watermelon.

Makes 2 sandwiches

Cooking Some Main-Dish Salad Basics

This is how to prepare moist simmered chicken, juicy shrimp, and perfect hard-cooked eggs.

Simmered Chicken for Salad
Step 1: **Cut up a 3- to 3½-pound frying chicken, *or* use 2 to 3 whole chicken breasts (2 to 3 lbs), halved. Place chicken pieces in a 4½- to 5-quart Dutch oven or deep frying pan. Add 1 teaspoon salt, ⅛ teaspoon dried thyme, ⅛ teaspoon whole peppercorns (white or black), 3 sprigs fresh parsley, 1 stalk celery (chopped), and 3 cups water.**
Step 2: **Bring to boiling over medium heat. Cover, reduce heat, and simmer just until chicken is tender (40 to 45 minutes for chicken pieces; 15 to 20 minutes for chicken breasts). Remove chicken from broth, reserving broth. (Strain and freeze for soups or sauces.) When chicken is cool enough to handle, remove and discard bones and skin.**
Step 3: **Dice or shred chicken into bite-size pieces. Makes 3 to 3½ cups cooked chicken.**

Cooked Shrimp for Salad
Step 1: **In a 3- to 4-quart saucepan or Dutch oven combine 2 cups water (use ½ cup dry white wine as part of the liquid, if you wish), 1 small onion (thinly sliced), 1 stalk celery (coarsely chopped), 1**

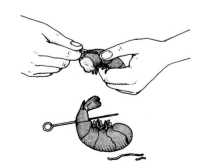

bay leaf, 3 sprigs fresh parsley, 1 teaspoon salt, ¼ teaspoon whole peppercorns (white or black), and 1 tablespoon lemon juice (or 2 to 3 slices fresh lemon). Bring to boiling. Cover, reduce heat, and simmer 5 minutes.**
Step 2: **Add 1 pound fresh shrimp (in shells). When mixture returns to boiling, remove pan from heat, cover, and let stand 10 minutes.**
Step 3: **Drain shrimp; peel and devein. Makes about 2 cups.**

Note: **If you wish to take the trouble, you can devein shrimp more neatly *before* they are cooked. Use a sharp, pointed bamboo skewer and insert it through the top of the shell in several places to lift out the sand vein. Shrimp will be moister and more flavorful if cooked in shells.**

Perfect Hard-Cooked Eggs
Step 1: **Place up to 6 eggs in a 2-quart saucepan and cover with cold water. Bring to boiling; then reduce heat so bubbles rise slowly to surface but do not break it. For tenderness and best color, the cooking water should *never boil* fully. Simmer for 20 minutes.**
Step 2: **Pour off water, cover eggs with cold water, and let stand, changing cold water occasionally, until eggs are cool (about 30 minutes).**

Deveining shrimp. To remove sand vein from shrimp in shell, use a sharp-pointed skewer (bamboo or metal). Insert it through the top of the shell to catch the vein and gently lift it out. If the vein breaks, you may need to pierce the shell in several places to remove all of the vein.

Open-Faced Guacamole Sandwiches

A leafy sandwich can be considered a salad. This one offers an abundance of vivid color and flavor contrasts.

8   slices sourdough rye bread
    Butter or margarine
8   slices Muenster or Monterey jack cheese, each about ¼ inch thick
    Guacamole (recipe follows)
1   large tomato, cut into 8 slices
8   sprigs cilantro
    Greek olives

1. Lightly butter bread on both sides; brown both sides on a griddle.
2. Top each slice of warm bread with cheese. Spread with guacamole.
3. Cut each tomato slice in half. Place 2 half slices on each sandwich. Top with cilantro. Add olives.

Makes 4 servings.

Guacamole
Halve, remove seeds, and peel 3 avocados. Mash with 2 tablespoons lime *or* lemon juice. Lightly mix in 1 clove garlic (minced or pressed), ¼ cup *each* finely chopped onion and chopped cilantro *or* parsley, ½ teaspoon salt, and a dash *each* Tabasco and pepper. Makes about 1½ cups.

Bountiful Bagel Sandwiches

Split bagels — toasted, if you like — make a good meatless sandwich.

2   tablespoons mayonnaise
1   tablespoon plain yogurt
1   teaspoon Dijon mustard
4   rye or onion bagels, split
4   tomato slices
¼   pound thinly sliced Swiss cheese
1   medium avocado, halved, peeled, seeded, and sliced
½   cup alfalfa sprouts

1. In a small bowl mix mayonnaise, yogurt, and mustard until smooth.
2. Spread cut surfaces of bagels with mayonnaise mixture. For each sandwich place (in order given) on bottom half of bagel a tomato slice, 1 ounce sliced Swiss cheese, a fourth of the avocado slices, and 2 tablespoons of the sprouts.
3. Add bagel tops; serve at once.

Makes 4 sandwiches.

Sandwich lunch with a dessert of homemade bar cookies awaits lunchtime conferees.

🐾 Lunch at the Conference Table

It often happens that department meetings continue through the lunch hour. Plan ahead and stimulate ideas with a menu of salad sandwiches brought from home, supplemented by simple relishes and home-baked cookies.

The crescents of pita bread are lined with a creamy mixture of *tahini* (ground sesame seed paste) and puréed garbanzos, then filled with a leafy salad.

Gingered Chicken Salad Sandwiches

Pocket Bread Salad Sandwiches

Cherry Tomatoes   Pickles

Layered Orange Bars

Raspberry-Filbert Bars

Bottled Water, Soft Drinks, or Carafe Wine

Coffee

Gingered Chicken Salad Sandwiches

3   cups diced cooked chicken
⅓   cup chopped toasted walnuts
1   stalk celery, finely chopped
⅓   cup *each* mayonnaise and
    sour cream
1   teaspoon *each* Dijon mustard,
    grated orange peel, and finely
    chopped preserved ginger
¼   teaspoon salt
12 slices raisin bread, toasted
    Butter or Boston lettuce leaves
    Orange wedges, for garnish

1. Lightly mix chicken, walnuts, and celery in a large bowl.
2. In a smaller bowl, mix until smooth mayonnaise, sour cream, mustard, orange peel, ginger, and salt. Add to chicken mixture, stirring to coat evenly. (If made ahead, cover and refrigerate to blend flavors.)
3. Spread chicken salad mixture evenly over each of 6 raisin toast slices, using a generous ½ cup filling for each. Cover with lettuce leaves and remaining toast slices. Cut each sandwich in halves or quarters. Garnish plates with orange wedges.

Makes 6 sandwiches.

Pocket Bread Salad Sandwiches

1   small can (8¾ oz) garbanzo
    beans, drained
1   clove garlic, minced or pressed
¼   cup plain yogurt
2   tablespoons lemon juice
¼   cup *tahini* (ground sesame
    seed paste)
6   pita (pocket) breads
2   cups torn red leaf lettuce
½   cup thinly sliced cucumber
1   small green pepper, seeded
    and chopped
¼   cup *each* slivered red onion
    and ripe olives
½   cup coarsely crumbled
    feta cheese
    Cumin Dressing (recipe follows)

1. In food processor or blender combine garbanzos, garlic, yogurt,

and lemon juice; process or whirl until smoothly puréed. Blend in *tahini.*
2. Wrap pita breads loosely in foil and heat in a 350°F oven for 10 to 15 minutes, until warm. Cut each in half to make 2 half-rounds.
3. While bread warms, lightly mix lettuce, cucumber, green pepper, red onion, olives, and cheese.
4. To serve, spread about 1 heaping tablespoon of the *tahini* mixture in each pita bread half. Lightly combine lettuce mixture and dressing. Divide salad filling evenly among pita bread halves. Serve at once.

Makes 6 servings.

Cumin Dressing

In a small bowl mix 1 tablespoon red wine vinegar, 1 teaspoon lemon juice, ¼ teaspoon *each* salt and ground cumin, and ⅛ teaspoon *each* paprika and dried oregano. Using a whisk or fork, gradually mix in ¼ cup olive oil. Makes about ⅓ cup.

Layered Orange Bars

⅓   cup butter or margarine,
    softened
¼   cup granulated sugar
2   teaspoons grated orange rind
1   cup plus 2 tablespoons
    all-purpose flour
1   egg
½   cup firmly packed brown sugar
½   teaspoon vanilla
¼   teaspoon baking powder
½   cup chopped walnuts
½   cup flaked coconut
    Orange Glaze (recipe follows)

1. For bottom layer, cream butter, sugar, and 1 teaspoon of the orange rind until fluffy. Gradually stir in 1 cup of the flour until mixture is crumbly. Press evenly and firmly over bottom of a greased 8-inch-square baking pan. Bake in a 350°F oven for 15 minutes.
2. Meanwhile, beat egg with brown sugar and vanilla until well blended. Mix in remaining 2 tablespoons flour, baking powder, and remaining 1 teaspoon orange rind. Then fold in walnuts and coconut. Spread coconut mixture over partially baked crust.

3. Return to 350°F oven and bake until well browned and set in center (18 to 20 minutes). Place pan on a rack. Drizzle glaze over warm cookies. When cool, cut into bars about 1¼ by 1¾ inches.

Makes 2 dozen cookies.

Orange Glaze

In a small bowl mix ⅔ cup powdered sugar, ½ teaspoon grated orange rind, and 1 to 1½ tablespoons orange juice until smooth.

Raspberry-Filbert Bars

½   cup (¼ lb) butter or margarine,
    softened
½   cup firmly packed light brown
    sugar
¼   cup granulated sugar
½   teaspoon vanilla
1   egg
⅔   cup ground filberts (whirled in
    blender or food processor until
    powdery)
1   teaspoon grated lemon rind
1½ cups all-purpose flour
½   teaspoon ground cinnamon
¼   teaspoon *each* salt, ground
    nutmeg, and ground cloves
¾   teaspoon baking powder
¾   cup red raspberry preserves
    Powdered sugar

1. In a large bowl cream butter, sugars, and vanilla until fluffy. Beat in egg until mixture is light colored. Mix in filberts and lemon rind. Stir flour with salt, spices, and baking powder; gradually add to butter mixture, beating slowly until combined. Wrap a third of the dough in plastic film and chill for 30 minutes.
2. With floured fingers press remaining dough evenly over bottom of a greased 8-inch-square baking pan. Spread with preserves. Divide chilled dough into 12 pieces; roll each on a floured surface to form an 8-inch strand. Arrange in a lattice pattern over preserves.
3. Bake in a 375°F oven until a deep golden brown (30 to 35 minutes). Sift powdered sugar lightly over top while warm. When cool, cut into bars about 1¼ by 1¾ inches.

Makes 2 dozen cookies.

Salads from Around the World

Salads are virtually an international enthusiasm. Indeed, the very word comes from the Latin *salata*. Many favorite salads originated in other lands and cultures.

In this chapter you will find a sampling of salad recipes from many cuisines. Their diversity underscores the many types of salads — green salads, vegetable salads, salads of grains and potatoes, main dish salads, and a menu featuring a French salad sandwich.

Smoked Salmon Rolls

In British Columbia, Canada, where salmon is plentiful and of superb quality, these cream-filled smoked salmon rolls on a bed of lettuce are a luxurious first course.

- ½ cup whipping cream
- 1 tablespoon lemon juice
- ⅛ teaspoon salt
  Pinch white pepper
- 1 tablespoon prepared horseradish
- ¼ pound small peeled, cooked shrimp
- 6 to 8 thin slices (about 6 oz) smoked salmon (lox)
  Shredded iceberg or romaine lettuce
  Lemon wedges, for garnish

Salad discoveries await the adventurous in all corners of the world. You can sample some of the delicious results of this culinary exploration in the pages that follow. The salad shown in the pink box is French pan bagnat *(recipe, page 87).*

1. Whip cream with lemon juice, salt, and pepper until stiff. Fold in horseradish and shrimp.
2. Place about 2 tablespoons of the cream mixture on each slice of salmon and roll each up carefully. Place, 2 rolls for each serving, on lettuce-lined plates. Garnish each with a lemon wedge.
Makes 3 to 4 servings.

German Herring Salad
(Schmandheringsalat)

Look for boneless herring pieces in a wine marinade to use in this German first-course salad. The fish is blanketed in a fluffy cream with onion, apple, and pickles.

- ½ cup whipping cream
  Pinch cayenne pepper
- ½ cup sour cream
- ⅓ cup slivered onion
- 1 tart apple, peeled, cored, and chopped
- ¼ cup chopped sour pickles
- 1 cup marinated herring fillets, well drained
  Butter or Boston lettuce
  Paprika, parsley sprigs, and tomato wedges, for garnish

1. Whip cream with cayenne until stiff. Fold in sour cream. Lightly mix in onion, apple, and pickles. Cover and refrigerate for 1 to 2 hours.
2. To serve, arrange herring fillets on lettuce leaves. Spoon whipped cream mixture over herring.
3. Sprinkle lightly with paprika; garnish with parsley and tomato.
Makes 4 servings.

Mexican Marinated Fish Salad
(Seviche)

Sea bass or other firm white fish, cut in cubes, "cooks" without heat in lime juice for several hours. Then tomato, avocado, and other flavorful seasonings are added to make a piquant seafood cocktail.

- 1 pound sea bass or other mild-flavored white fish fillets, cut in ½-inch cubes
- ⅓ cup lime *or* lemon juice
- ¼ cup chopped canned green chiles
- 3 green onions, thinly sliced
- 1 medium tomato, peeled, seeded, and chopped
- ½ teaspoon salt
- ⅛ teaspoon dried oregano
- 1 tablespoon olive oil
- 2 tablespoons chopped fresh cilantro (Chinese parsley) *or* parsley
- 1 medium avocado, halved and pitted
  Lime wedges for garnish

1. Place fish in a glass bowl. Mix lightly with lime juice. Cover and refrigerate for several hours or overnight, until fish is white and opaque, stirring occasionally.
2. About 2 hours before serving, mix in remaining ingredients except avocado and lime wedges; cover and refrigerate.
3. Cut avocado into small balls, using a melon ball cutter; mix lightly into fish mixture. Serve in seafood cocktail or sherbet dishes, garnished with lime wedges.

Makes 6 servings.

Marinated Eggplant Salad

Sicilian in origin, this eggplant salad is served at room temperature with tomatoes and ripe olives.

1 medium eggplant (about 1½ lbs), unpeeled
Salted water
¼ cup red wine vinegar
2 cloves garlic, minced or pressed
½ teaspoon salt
¼ teaspoon *each* dried basil, oregano, and crumbled rosemary
⅛ teaspoon coarsely ground black pepper
½ cup olive oil (or ¼ cup *each* olive oil and salad oil)
1 small, mild red onion, thinly sliced and separated into rings
¼ cup chopped fresh parsley
Sliced tomatoes and oil-cured black olives, for garnish

1. Cut eggplant into ½-inch cubes. Add to a large quantity of boiling salted water in a large, deep saucepan. Boil gently, uncovered, stirring occasionally, until tender (6 to 8 minutes). Drain well.
2. In a medium bowl mix vinegar, garlic, salt, basil, oregano, rosemary, and pepper. Using a fork or whisk, gradually beat in olive oil until well combined. Pour over eggplant in a large bowl; add onion and let stand at room temperature for about 1 hour.
3. Just before serving, mix in parsley. Mound eggplant mixture on a serving plate and circle with tomato slices. Garnish with olives.

Makes 6 to 8 servings.

Crispy Carrot Salad
(Carottes aux Noix)

Lemon accents this French first-course salad.

4 medium carrots, shredded (about 3 cups)
½ cup chopped toasted walnuts
2 tablespoons snipped fresh chives *or* chopped parsley
Lemon-Tarragon Dressing (recipe follows)
Butter or Boston lettuce leaves

1. Lightly mix carrots, walnuts, chives, and dressing. Cover and refrigerate for 1 to 3 hours to blend flavors.
2. Serve carrot mixture on lettuce leaves.

Makes 4 to 6 servings.

Lemon-Tarragon Dressing

In a small bowl mix 1 tablespoon *each* lemon juice and tarragon wine vinegar, 1 teaspoon Dijon mustard, ½ teaspoon grated lemon rind, ¼ teaspoon salt, and a pinch of white pepper. Using a whisk or fork, gradually beat in 1 tablespoon walnut oil or olive oil and ¼ cup salad oil until well combined. Makes about ½ cup.

Swiss Cheese Salad
(Salade de Gruyère)

From the French-speaking part of Switzerland comes this nippy salad of cubed cheese with pickled onions. Serve it either as a first course or as an accompaniment to baked ham or turkey.

2 cups diced Gruyère or Emmenthal cheese (about ½ lb), in ¼-inch cubes
1 stalk celery, finely chopped
⅓ cup drained small pickled onions
Creamy Mustard Dressing (recipe follows)
Butter or Boston lettuce leaves
Snipped fresh chives *or* chopped parsley, for garnish

1. Lightly mix cheese, celery, onions, and dressing. Cover and refrigerate for 1 to 3 hours to blend flavors.
2. Serve cheese mixture on lettuce leaves, sprinkled with chives.

Makes 4 servings.

Creamy Mustard Dressing

In a medium bowl mix 1 egg yolk, 1½ tablespoons tarragon wine vinegar, 1½ teaspoons Dijon mustard, a dash of cayenne pepper, and 1 clove garlic (minced or pressed). Using a whisk or fork, gradually beat in ⅓ cup olive oil until dressing is thick and creamy. Makes about ½ cup.

Mushrooms à la Grecque

The French designation *à la grecque* usually refers to vegetables that have been cooked in oil and vinegar and then cooled and served at room temperature. As such, these mushrooms are a nice hors d'oeuvre (served with cocktail picks) or first-course salad.

1 pound small whole mushrooms (or quartered mushrooms, if large)
½ cup olive oil
2 cloves garlic, minced or pressed
1 teaspoon salt
⅛ teaspoon white pepper
½ teaspoon dried thyme leaves
1 teaspoon grated lemon rind
1 bay leaf
Juice of 1 large lemon (about 3 Tbsp)
¼ cup tarragon vinegar
Chopped parsley, for garnish

1. Rinse mushrooms and pat dry. Cook mushrooms for 3 minutes in heated olive oil in a frying pan, stirring constantly over medium heat.
2. Mix in garlic, salt, pepper, thyme, lemon rind, bay leaf, lemon juice, and vinegar. Boil gently, stirring frequently, for 3 minutes.
3. Transfer mushrooms and their liquid to a glass bowl. Cool; then cover and chill if made ahead.
4. Serve at room temperature, sprinkled with parsley.

Makes 4 to 6 servings.

Celery Root Salad
(Céléri Rémoulade)

The unglamorous vegetable, celery root, when peeled and shredded, can be transformed into an elegant French salad. A creamy mustard-and-shallot dressing helps. (Use your food processor, if you have one, for the tedious shredding job.)

1 large celery root (1 to 1½ lbs)
2 tablespoons lemon juice
1 egg yolk
2 tablespoons tarragon wine vinegar
1 tablespoon Dijon mustard
½ teaspoon salt
Pinch cayenne pepper

Ordering hors d'oeuvre variés *in a French restaurant might bring forth an assortment such as this. Clockwise from top right are Mushrooms à la Grecque, Crispy Carrot Salad (both recipes are on page 80), Dilled Cucumbers (recipe below), Celery Root Salad, and Swiss Cheese Salad (both on page 80). The salad of julienne beets at top left is part of the Black Forest-style salad plate for which the recipe appears below, but it has character enough to be served apart from that combination.*

1   shallot, finely chopped
¼   cup *each* olive oil and salad oil
      Butter or Boston lettuce leaves
      Chopped fresh parsley

1. Peel celery root thoroughly, cutting out any deep bits of peel. Shred quickly, using a food processor or grater. (You should have 5 to 6 cups.) Immediately mix well with lemon juice to prevent discoloration. Cover and refrigerate for about 1 hour.
2. In a medium bowl beat egg yolk with vinegar, mustard, salt, cayenne, and shallot. Using a whisk or fork, gradually beat in olive and salad oils until dressing is thick and creamy.

3. Shortly before serving, mix celery root lightly with dressing.
4. Serve celery root mixture on lettuce leaves, sprinkled with parsley.
Makes 6 servings

Ham and Salad Plate, Black Forest–Style

Three vegetable salads complement sliced baked ham—warm or cold—to make a typical German supper with light rye bread.

1   small can (8¼ oz) julienne beets, well drained
¼   teaspoon caraway seeds
      Sweet-Sour Dressing (recipe follows)
3   medium carrots, shredded

2   tablespoons chopped fresh parsley
1   to 1½ pounds sliced baked ham, warm or cold
      Butter or Boston lettuce
      Dilled Cucumbers (recipe follows)
      Sharp German-style mustard

1. In a medium bowl lightly mix beets, caraway seeds, and about a third of the dressing. In another bowl lightly mix carrots, parsley, and remaining dressing. Cover both bowls and refrigerate for 1 to 3 hours to blend flavors.
2. To serve, arrange ham slices on each of 4 plates lined with lettuce leaves. To each plate, add a serving of each of the 3 salads: beets, carrots, and cucumbers.
3. Accompany with mustard.
Makes 4 servings.

Sweet-Sour Dressing
In a small bowl mix 2 tablespoons white wine vinegar, 2 teaspoons coarse-grained German or Dijon mustard, ½ teaspoon sugar, ¼ teaspoon salt, and a pinch of white pepper. Using a whisk or fork, gradually beat in ⅓ cup salad oil until well combined. Makes ½ cup.

Dilled Cucumbers

Peel 1 medium cucumber if skin is tough or waxed. Slice very thinly. Sprinkle slices lightly with salt. Place in a colander and let stand 15 minutes; press lightly to remove moisture. Transfer slices to a bowl. Add 1 tablespoon sugar, 2 tablespoons white vinegar, ½ teaspoon salt, and ¼ teaspoon dried dill weed; mix lightly. Cover and refrigerate for 1 to 3 hours to blend flavors.

Makes 4 servings.

Chicken livers are featured in a walnut-sprinkled French first-course salad.

Green Salad with Chicken Livers
(Salade Bressane)

This salad was inspired by one created by Jean-Paul Lacombe, the inventive young chef of the restaurant Léon de Lyon in France's gastronomic heartland. In Lyon, the chicken livers can come from choice Bresse chickens; elsewhere, poaching the livers in cream with mustard compensates for a more humble origin. Serve this salad as the first course of a French dinner.

½ pound chicken livers
⅓ cup whipping cream
1 teaspoon Dijon mustard
¼ teaspoon salt
  Pinch white pepper
3 cups *each* bite-size pieces of torn Australian *or* green leaf lettuce and tender young chicory
  Walnut Oil Dressing (recipe follows)
1 hard-cooked egg, chopped
¼ cup coarsely chopped toasted walnuts

1. Drain chicken livers and pat dry. In a medium frying pan mix cream, mustard, salt, and pepper. Bring to boiling over medium-high heat, stirring until cream is reduced by about a third. Mix in livers, stirring gently to coat with cream. Reduce heat to medium and cook, turning carefully occasionally, until liquid is reduced to a glaze that clings to livers. Remove from heat and let stand until livers are barely warm.
2. In a large bowl combine greens. Mix lightly with dressing. Divide greens among 4 salad plates. Sprinkle each serving with a fourth of the egg and a fourth of the walnuts.
3. Cut chicken livers into ¼-inch slices; arrange overlapping slices beside each serving of salad. Serve at once.

Makes 4 servings.

Walnut Oil Dressing

In a medium bowl mix 1 tablespoon *each* red wine vinegar and lemon juice, 1 teaspoon Dijon mustard, ¼ teaspoon salt, and ⅛ teaspoon white pepper. Using a whisk or fork, gradually beat in 2 tablespoons *each* olive oil and walnut oil until dressing is slightly thickened and well combined. Makes about ⅓ cup.

Italian Mixed Green Salad
(Insalata Mista)

The artistry of Italian salad-makers is limited only by the variety of fresh greens and other vegetables at the day's market. Here is a typical combination, colorful yet simple. It can be made with a mixture of fresh young garden greens to make 6 cups, lightly packed. If possible, include about 1 cup arugula in the assortment.

6 cups torn green leaf lettuce
1 small sweet red or yellow bell pepper, seeded and slivered
½ cup thinly slivered fresh fennel bulb *or* celery
  Olive Oil Vinaigrette Dressing (recipe follows)
1 medium tomato, cut in wedges
1 small carrot, shredded

1. Place lettuce, pepper, and fennel in a large salad bowl.
2. Mix lightly with dressing. Arrange tomato wedges in center of salad. Sprinkle with shredded carrot.

Makes 4 to 6 servings.

Olive Oil Vinaigrette Dressing

In a small bowl mix 1 tablespoon *each* balsamic *or* sherry wine vinegar and lemon juice, 1 small clove garlic (minced or pressed), ¼ teaspoon salt, and a pinch of pepper. Using a whisk or fork, gradually beat in ⅓ cup olive oil until well combined. Makes about 6 tablespoons dressing.

Les Halles Spinach Salad

This fresh spinach salad is inspired by the fare of bistros clustered around what was once the wholesale food market of Paris. Sliced mushrooms, tomatoes, and tiny cubes of Swiss cheese complement the greens.

1 bunch (about ¾ lb) spinach
  Creamy Mustard Dressing (recipe follows)
6 ounces mushrooms, thinly sliced
1 tomato, cut into 8 wedges
½ cup diced Swiss cheese (about ¼-in. cubes)
2 hard-cooked eggs, grated

1. Remove and discard stems from spinach; you should have about 6 cups leaves. Mix lightly with about two-thirds of the dressing; arrange on 4 salad plates.
2. Arrange mushrooms in rows on opposite sides of each portion of spinach. Place tomato wedges along other sides. Drizzle remaining dressing over mushrooms and tomatoes.
3. Scatter cheese cubes over spinach. Sprinkle grated eggs over cheese. Serve at once.

Makes 4 servings.

Creamy Mustard Dressing

Beat 1 egg yolk with 2 tablespoons sherry wine vinegar, 1 teaspoon Dijon mustard, ¼ teaspoon *each* salt and dried tarragon, and a dash of freshly ground black pepper. Using a whisk or fork, gradually beat in ¼ cup *each* olive oil and salad oil. Makes about ⅔ cup.

Russian Potato Salad

Beets tint this dill-accented potato salad a pleasant pink color and also give it an earthy sweetness.

1½ pounds (about 9) small new potatoes
    Salted water
¼ cup white vinegar
1½ teaspoons salt
¾ teaspoon dried dill weed
⅛ teaspoon white pepper
¼ cup salad oil
4 hard-cooked eggs
1 can (1 lb) julienne beets, well drained
6 green onions, thinly sliced
1 tablespoon drained capers
2 teaspoons Dijon mustard
1 tablespoon prepared horseradish
½ cup sour cream
    Chopped fresh parsley, for garnish

1. Cook potatoes (unpeeled) in boiling salted water to cover until tender (25 to 30 minutes). Drain, slip off skins, and cut into ½-inch cubes while warm. (You should have about 6 cups.) Place in a large bowl.
2. While potatoes cook, in a small bowl mix 3 tablespoons of the vinegar, salt, dill weed, and white pepper. Using a whisk or fork, gradually beat in oil until well combined. Pour oil mixture over warm potatoes, stirring gently to combine. Cover and refrigerate for at least 2 hours (or as long as overnight, if you wish).
3. Chop 2 of the hard-cooked eggs; add to potatoes. Cut remaining eggs into halves, reserving yolks. Chop whites and add to potatoes with beets, green onions, and capers.
4. For dressing, mash or sieve reserved egg yolks in a medium bowl. Mix in remaining 1 tablespoon vinegar, mustard, and horseradish until well combined. Mix in sour cream until smooth. Fold dressing into potato mixture. Cover and refrigerate for 1 to 3 hours to blend flavors. Mix lightly, then garnish with parsley.

Makes 6 servings.

Green Salad with Guacamole

Here is the perfect introduction to a Mexican feast: a mixed green salad topped generously with the perky avocado concoction, guacamole. For best flavor, mash soft-ripe avocados so that they remain slightly chunky — the mixture should not be perfectly smooth.

4 cups *each* shredded iceberg lettuce and romaine
2 tablespoons white wine vinegar
2 teaspoons lime *or* lemon juice
1 teaspoon Dijon mustard
½ clove garlic, minced or pressed
¼ teaspoon *each* salt and dried oregano
    Dash seasoned pepper
¼ cup *each* olive oil and salad oil
    Guacamole (recipe follows)
1 cup cherry tomatoes

1. Lightly mix lettuce and romaine in a large bowl.
2. In a medium bowl mix vinegar, lime juice, mustard, garlic, salt, oregano, and pepper. Using a whisk or fork, gradually mix in oils until well blended and slightly thickened. Mix dressing lightly with greens.
3. Divide greens evenly among 4 to 6 individual salad plates. Spoon guacamole in a mound in center of each serving. Garnish with tomatoes.

Makes 4 to 6 servings.

Guacamole

Halve, seed, and peel 2 ripe avocados. Mash with 1 tablespoon lime juice until mixture is soft but still chunky. Lightly mix in 3 sliced green onions, 2 tablespoons chopped fresh cilantro (Chinese parsley) *or* parsley, ¼ teaspoon salt, and a dash *each* Tabasco sauce and seasoned pepper. Makes about 1½ cups.

The chunky avocado mixture known in Mexico as guacamole *makes a green salad a feast.*

Deftly mix Greek Spinach Salad at the table.

Chicken, Ham, and Spiced Cheese Salad

The Dutch spiced cheese, Leyden, may be flavored with caraway seeds, cloves, or cumin seeds. Any of these varieties complement chicken and ham in this Dutch main dish salad. If you are unable to obtain Leyden cheese, use Kuminost or another spiced type.

3 cups cubed or shredded cooked chicken (see page 75)
1 cup julienne strips baked ham
½ cup diced spiced cheese (about ¼-in. cubes), such as Leyden or Kuminost
1 egg yolk
1 tablespoon peach wine vinegar *or* white wine vinegar
2 teaspoons Dijon mustard
Dash cayenne pepper
⅓ cup salad oil
1 green onion, thinly sliced
Shredded romaine
Tomato and hard-cooked egg wedges, for garnish

1. In a large bowl, combine chicken, ham, and cheese.
2. In a medium bowl beat egg yolk with vinegar, mustard, and cayenne. Using a fork or whisk, gradually beat in salad oil until thick and creamy. Mix in green onion.
3. Lightly mix dressing with chicken mixture. If made ahead, cover and refrigerate. Serve on shredded romaine on 4 to 6 individual salad plates. Garnish with tomatoes and eggs.

Makes 4 to 6 servings.

Minted Wheat Salad (*Tabbuli*)

Fresh mint and parsley make this Middle Eastern salad memorable. Use your food processor to make quick work of chopping the fresh herbs. This salad makes a good hors d'oeuvre; use tender inner leaves of romaine to scoop up the mixture.

1 cup bulgur wheat
  Water
⅓ cup lemon juice
1 teaspoon salt
⅛ teaspoon pepper
⅔ cup olive oil
½ cup *each* thinly sliced green onions and finely chopped parsley
⅓ cup chopped fresh mint leaves
1 medium tomato, seeded and chopped
  Inner romaine leaves

1. Rinse bulgur and drain well. Cover with cold water and let stand for 1 hour. Drain well, pressing out moisture.
2. In a large bowl mix lemon juice, salt, and pepper. Using a whisk or fork, gradually beat in oil until well combined. To oil mixture add drained bulgur, green onions, parsley, and mint; mix lightly. Cover and refrigerate until ready to serve (at least 2 hours).
3. Mound *tabbuli* in a shallow serving dish; sprinkle with tomato. Surround with romaine leaves, to use as scoops for serving and eating.

Makes 4 to 6 servings.

Greek Spinach Salad with Hot Oil Dressing

Fragrant olive oil, heated just enough to release its aroma, dresses this spinach salad with onion, olives, and feta cheese. It can be served as a first course for 4, or a luncheon main dish for 2.

1 bunch (about ¾ lb) spinach
½ cup *each* slivered mild red onion, whole Greek olives, and crumbled feta cheese
1 tablespoon sherry wine vinegar
¼ teaspoon dried oregano
1 small clove garlic, minced or pressed
⅛ teaspoon salt
3 tablespoons olive oil
  Baguette Croutons (recipe follows)
  Coarsely ground black pepper

1. Remove and discard stems from spinach; you should have about 8 cups leaves. Place spinach in salad bowl with onion, olives, and cheese.
2. In a small bowl combine vinegar, oregano, garlic, and salt.
3. In a small pan swirl olive oil over medium heat until it is just warm to touch (2 to 3 minutes). Using a whisk or fork, gradually beat hot oil into vinegar mixture.
4. Lightly and quickly mix hot dressing with spinach mixture. Gently stir in croutons. Serve at once, offering freshly ground pepper to taste.

Makes 4 servings.

Baguette Croutons
Slice a *baguette* (long, thin loaf of French bread) crosswise to make 24 thin slices. In a small pan over medium heat melt 2 tablespoons butter or margarine; add 1 tablespoon olive oil and 1 small clove garlic (minced or pressed). Place bread slices in a single layer on a baking sheet. Brush with butter mixture. Bake in a 250°F oven until crisp and lightly browned (25 to 30 minutes).

Seafood Fiesta Tostada

Crisp flour tortilla bowls make a dramatic setting for a generous Mexican shrimp and crab salad.

Flour Tortilla Bowls (directions follow)
4   large leaves green leaf lettuce
8   cups shredded iceberg lettuce
½   cup sliced radishes
Garlic Dressing (recipe follows)
Avocado Mixture (recipe follows)
1   pound shrimp, cooked, shelled, and deveined (see page 75)
½   pound cooked crabmeat, flaked
2   hard-cooked eggs, cut in wedges
Lemon or lime slices, ripe olives, tomato wedges, cucumber sticks, carrot curls, and paprika, for garnish

1. Place tortilla bowls on a leaf of lettuce on each of 4 large salad plates.
2. Lightly mix shredded lettuce, radishes, and dressing; divide evenly among tortilla bowls. Top each with a dollop of avocado mixture; then surround avocado with shrimp. Cover with crab.
3. Garnish with egg wedges, lemon slices, olives, tomato, cucumber, and carrot; sprinkle crab lightly with paprika.

Makes 4 servings.

Flour Tortilla Bowls

Pour salad oil into a large frying pan to a depth of ½ inch; heat to 375°F. Fry four 8- to 9-inch-diameter flour tortillas, one at a time for about 45 seconds, turning carefully with 2 spatulas, until bubbly and just golden but still flexible. Remove to a metal colander or wire strainer lined with paper towels and gently form into a bowl shape; when cool, remove and set aside. Repeat for remaining tortillas.

Garlic Dressing

In a small bowl combine 2 tablespoons lime *or* lemon juice; ⅛ teaspoon *each* salt, seasoned pepper, and ground cumin; and 1 clove garlic (minced or pressed). With a whisk or fork gradually beat in ⅓ cup olive oil or salad oil. Makes about 6 tablespoons dressing.

Avocado Mixture

Halve, seed, and peel 2 ripe avocados. Mash with 1 tablespoon lime juice until mixture is soft but still chunky. Lightly mix in ¼ cup sliced green onions, 2 tablespoons fresh cilantro (Chinese parsley) *or* parsley, ¼ teaspoon salt, and a dash *each* Tabasco sauce and seasoned pepper. Makes about 1½ cups.

Asparagus Pont-Aven

This elegant fresh asparagus in a mustardy vinaigrette dressing is prepared in the style of a lovely village in Brittany. It is most appealing if the asparagus is served slightly warm.

2   tablespoons *each* white wine vinegar and lemon juice
¼   teaspoon salt
2   teaspoons Dijon mustard
⅛   teaspoon *each* white pepper and dried tarragon
¼   cup olive oil
½   cup salad oil
2 to 3   pounds asparagus
Butter or Boston lettuce leaves
2   hard-cooked eggs, shredded

1. For dressing, combine in a medium bowl vinegar, lemon juice, salt, mustard, pepper, and tarragon. Using a whisk or fork, gradually beat in olive oil and salad oil until smooth and well combined.
2. Snap off fibrous ends of asparagus; peel remainder of stem, if you wish. Steam over boiling water, or cook in a single layer in a broad, shallow pan in a small amount of boiling salted water until tender-crisp (6 to 8 minutes). Drain well.
3. Arrange warm asparagus spears in 6 individual shallow au gratin dishes. Tuck a butter lettuce leaf under each serving of asparagus. Beat dressing to combine well; pour evenly over each serving of asparagus. Sprinkle with shredded hard-cooked eggs.

Makes 6 servings.

This French creation of fresh asparagus is cooked tender-crisp and served while still warm. Bathed in an oil-and-vinegar dressing and topped with shredded, hard-cooked eggs, it makes an elegant luncheon dish.

Chinese Chicken Salad

The puffy-crisp rice noodles (or sticks) that add so much appeal to this distinctive salad are sometimes labeled with their Chinese name, *mai fun*. Look for them in stores specializing in Oriental foods. When you fry them, be sure the oil is heated to the temperature specified, for maximum volume and crispness.

2   tablespoons sesame seeds
2   whole chicken breasts (4 halves, about 2 lbs), boned and skinned
    Salt
1   tablespoon *each* Oriental sesame oil and salad oil
    Hoisin Dressing (recipe follows)
    Rice sticks (directions for frying follow)
4   cups shredded iceberg lettuce
4   green onions, thinly sliced
½   cup coarsely chopped fresh cilantro (Chinese parsley)

1. Stir sesame seeds in a small frying pan over medium heat until lightly browned (6 to 8 minutes); set aside.
2. Pound chicken breasts between pieces of waxed paper, using the flat side of a meat mallet, to a thickness of about ¼ inch. Cut into bite-size strips about ½ inch wide. Salt.

3. In mixture of heated oils in a wok or large frying pan brown half the chicken lightly, stirring and turning over medium-high heat until cooked through (about 3 minutes); remove from pan. Add remaining chicken and cook in the same way.
4. Mix chicken with Hoisin Dressing and let stand while assembling salad.
5. Prepare rice sticks as directed and set aside.
6. In a large bowl or deep platter mix lettuce, green onions, and cilantro. Add chicken and dressing, sesame seeds, and rice sticks and mix lightly. Serve at once.

Makes 4 servings.

Hoisin Dressing

In a small bowl mix 2 tablespoons *each* hoisin sauce and lemon juice and 2 teaspoons sugar. Using a whisk or fork, gradually beat in 1 tablespoon Oriental sesame oil and 3 tablespoons salad oil. Makes about ½ cup.

To fry rice sticks: Pour salad oil into a wok or large, deep frying pan to a depth of about 2 inches; heat to 350°F. Add a generous handful of rice sticks. Stir and fry just until puffy and crisp (15 to 30 seconds). Remove from fat and drain well. You should have about 2 cups.

Molded Ham and Parsley Salad
(*Jambon Persillé*)

A specialty of the Burgundy region of France, this ham salad makes a nice hot weather main dish. You might accompany it with a salad of cooked red and white kidney beans, chopped tomatoes, and a light oil-and-vinegar dressing.

2   envelopes unflavored gelatin
½   cup cold water
2   cans (13¾ oz *each*) chicken broth
4   cups coarsely chopped baked or simmered ham, fat and skin removed
2   tablespoons tarragon wine vinegar
2   cloves garlic, minced or pressed
1   shallot *or* 2 green onions, finely chopped
⅛   teaspoon *each* ground cloves and allspice
½   cup finely chopped fresh parsley
    Butter or Boston lettuce
    Radishes, for garnish

1. Sprinkle gelatin over water in a medium saucepan; let stand 5 minutes. Place over medium heat, stirring until gelatin dissolves. Remove from heat and mix in chicken broth. Refrigerate, stirring occasionally, until mixture begins to thicken.
2. Meanwhile, lightly mix ham, vinegar, garlic, shallot, cloves, and allspice in a 7- to 8-cup bowl or charlotte mold. Cover and refrigerate until ready to add gelatin mixture.
3. Mix parsley into slightly thickened gelatin mixture. Pour over ham, mixing lightly to blend. Refrigerate until firm (at least 6 hours —or overnight, if you wish).
4. Unmold, or serve by spoonfuls from bowl, on lettuce-lined platter or individual plates. Garnish with radishes.

Makes 6 servings.

The melt-in-the-mouth crunchiness of the puffy-crisp rice noodles called mai fun *is an irresistible feature of this popular Chinese Chicken Salad. Look for the noodles in stores that feature Oriental foods.*

Pan Bagnat
Deviled Eggs Provençal
Radishes   Thick Potato Chips
Bite-Size Lemon Tarts
Dry Rosé Wine   Coffee

🌿 *Provençal Beach Picnic*

For picnics in the south of France, the ingredients of a leafy *salade Niçoise* are heaped on French rolls to make healthy tuna sandwiches.

Although the French enjoy these sandwiches made ahead, that results in rather soggy rolls and limp lettuce. For a crisper sandwich, carry the salad mixture and other elements separately. Then add dressing and assemble the sandwiches when you are ready to eat.

Provençal Salad-in-a-Sandwich (Pan Bagnat)

3   cups torn butter or Boston lettuce
⅓   cup slivered red onion
¼   cup small whole Niçoise *or* slivered black olives
1   stalk celery, thinly sliced
1   small green pepper, seeded and slivered
    Niçoise Dressing (recipe follows)
4   large round or rectangular French rolls, split
1   can (6½ oz) chunk light tuna, drained
1   tomato, thinly sliced

1. Lightly mix lettuce, onion, olives, celery, green pepper, and dressing.
2. Place about a fourth of the lettuce mixture on bottom half of each roll. Cover each with a fourth of the tuna and tomato slices. Add tops of rolls.

Makes 4 sandwiches.

Niçoise Dressing

In a small bowl combine 2 tablespoons red wine vinegar, 1 small clove garlic (minced or pressed), ¼ teaspoon salt, and ⅛ teaspoon dried *herbes de Provence*. Using a whisk or fork, gradually beat in ⅓ cup olive oil, mixing until well combined. Makes about 6 tablespoons.

It's off to the beach for a picnic of French salad sandwiches with lemon dessert tarts.

Deviled Eggs Provençal

4   hard-cooked eggs (see page 75)
3   tablespoons mayonnaise
1½ teaspoons anchovy paste
1   teaspoon Dijon mustard
2   tablespoons finely chopped green pepper

1. Cut eggs in halves lengthwise. Remove yolks to a bowl, reserving whites.
2. Mash egg yolks; mix smoothly with mayonnaise, anchovy paste, and mustard. Mix in green pepper.
3. Mound egg yolk mixture in egg whites. Cover and refrigerate until ready to serve (up to 8 hours).

Makes 4 servings.

Bite-size Lemon Tarts

½   cup (¼ lb) butter or margarine, softened
1   small package (3 oz) cream cheese, softened
2   tablespoons powdered sugar
1   tablespoon brandy
1¼ cups all-purpose flour
    Lemon Filling (recipe follows)

1. Cream butter, cream cheese, and powdered sugar until light and fluffy. Beat in brandy. Gradually mix in flour until dough is smooth.
2. Divide dough evenly into 24 small muffin cups about 1½ inches in diameter. With fingertips press pastry evenly into pans. Pierce each shell with a fork in several places.
3. Bake in a 350°F oven until golden brown (18 to 20 minutes). Cool in pans on wire racks.
4. Fill with Lemon Filling. Serve cold or at room temperature.

Makes 2 dozen small tarts.

Lemon Filling

In top of a double boiler melt ¼ cup butter or margarine over direct heat. Remove from heat and add 1 teaspoon grated lemon peel, ¼ cup lemon juice, ⅔ cup sugar, and 2 eggs, beating until smooth. Place over simmering water and cook, stirring frequently, until thickened and smooth (about 20 minutes). Let stand until cool. Makes about 1 cup.

Salad Dressings

The perfect finishing touch for most salads is a skillfully executed dressing — a light, flavorful gilding of the greens moments before the salad is served.

Each of the salads in this book has been paired with an appropriate dressing, many of which you will enjoy with salads of your own creation. To encourage you to begin inventing your own superb dressings, the recipes in this chapter illustrate the basic principles for making the fundamental dressings.

First comes the oil-and-vinegar dressing, or *vinaigrette*. By selecting from an ever-expanding supply of different sorts of oils and vinegars (page 94), you can achieve astonishing variations in flavor.

Creamy dressings usually start with *mayonnaise,* a thick, silken emulsion of oil in eggs. Making your own mayonnaise at home takes no more than 2 egg yolks, a bit of vinegar and other flavorings, and 1 cup of oil—and a lot of wrist action. Equally as delicious a result can be achieved with much less work using an electric mixer, blender, or food processor. Such popular dressings as Thousand Island, Green Goddess, and blue cheese all begin with mayonnaise.

Remember this handy rule: For a green salad with about 2 quarts of greens, you will need about ⅓ cup of an oil-and-vinegar dressing and from ⅓ to ½ cup of a creamy one.

These days salad makers can choose oils and vinegars for dressings from an exotic selection – look into French fruit vinegars, special olive oils (more on page 94).

Basic Oil-and-Vinegar Dressing

Here is the elementary dressing that serves most green salads so well. As you will see, it welcomes innovative variations.

The flavor of the standard dressing is quite mild. You may wish to strengthen it by adding to the vinegar mixture before beating in oils 1 clove garlic (minced or pressed) or 1 shallot (finely chopped). For a creamier, more pungently flavored dressing, increase the Dijon mustard to as much as 1 tablespoon. Using other oils or vinegars (page 94) will also produce subtle flavor variations.

2 tablespoons wine vinegar
1 teaspoon Dijon mustard *or* ¼ teaspoon dry mustard
¼ teaspoon salt
    Pinch pepper
6 tablespoons (⅓ cup + 2 tsp.) olive oil or salad oil (or mixture of the two)

1. In a small bowl mix vinegar, mustard, salt, and pepper.
2. Using a whisk or fork, gradually beat in oil until dressing is slightly thickened and well combined. If made ahead, beat again to combine thoroughly before adding to salad.
Makes just under ½ cup.

Herbed Dressing

To vinegar mixture add 1 small clove garlic (minced or pressed) and ⅛ teaspoon *each* dried basil and summer savory. After beating in oil mix in 1 tablespoon *each* chopped fresh parsley and snipped fresh chives.

Curry Dressing

To vinegar mixture add 1 small clove garlic (minced or pressed) and ½ teaspoon curry powder; then beat in oil.

Anchovy Dressing

Omit salt from vinegar mixture; add 1 teaspoon anchovy paste and 1 small clove garlic (minced or pressed). After beating in oil, mix in 1 tablespoon chopped fresh parsley.

Sweet-Sour Dressing

To vinegar mixture add 2 teaspoons tomato paste, ½ teaspoon *each* sugar and Worcestershire sauce, and ⅛ teaspoon ground ginger; then beat in oil.

Ginger-Lemon Dressing

Use 1 tablespoon *each* lemon juice and white wine vinegar in place of the 2 tablespoons wine vinegar; omit mustard. To vinegar, salt, and pepper add 1 teaspoon grated fresh ginger and ½ teaspoon grated lemon rind; then beat in oil.

Dill Dressing

To vinegar mixture add 1 small clove garlic (minced or pressed) and ¼ teaspoon dried dill weed; then beat in oil.

Mayonnaise I

The proportions of this golden mayonnaise are tailored to beating the mixture by hand (using a balloon-shaped wire whisk) or with an electric mixer. Adding the oil drop by drop at the beginning, until about a third of it has been incorporated, requires patience but is necessary for a smoothly blended final product.

2   egg yolks, at room temperature
2   teaspoons Dijon mustard
¼   teaspoon salt
⅛   teaspoon *each* paprika and white pepper
2   tablespoons white wine vinegar
¼   cup olive oil (optional)
¾   cup salad oil (if olive oil is omitted, increase salad oil to 1 cup)

1. Fill deep, medium-size bowl (or electric mixer bowl) with hot water and let stand a few minutes. Pour out water; dry bowl well; and add egg yolks, mustard, salt, paprika, pepper, and 1 tablespoon of the vinegar. Mix to blend.
2. Slowly, adding oil drop-by-drop at first, beat in oil at high speed, using wire whisk or electric beaters. When about a third of the oil has been added, increase speed of addition, dribbling in oil in a thin, steady steam. Continue beating until all oil has been added and mayonnaise is thick and smooth.
3. Beat in remaining 1 tablespoon vinegar.

Makes about 1¼ cups.

Mayonnaise II

When you make mayonnaise in a blender or food processor, you can use the whole egg. All mayonnaises should be kept in the refrigerator, because the egg content makes them perishable.

1   egg
2   teaspoons Dijon mustard
¼   teaspoon salt
⅛   teaspoon *each* paprika and white pepper
2   tablespoons white wine vinegar
¼   cup olive oil (optional)

You can make perfect mayonnaise, mixed by hand – and the flavor is worth the work.

¾   cup salad oil (if olive oil is omitted, increase salad oil to 1 cup)

1. In blender container or food processor (with metal blade) combine egg, mustard, salt, paprika, pepper, and vinegar.
2. Cover and turn on blender or food processor. *Immediately* begin pouring in the oil in a very slow, steady steam. Whirl or process until thick and smooth.

Makes about 1¼ cups.

Lemon Mayonnaise

Decrease mustard to 1 teaspoon; increase salt to ½ teaspoon; in place of white wine vinegar use 1 tablespoon *each* lemon juice and tarragon wine vinegar. To egg mixture add 1½ teaspoons grated lemon rind and 1 small clove garlic (minced or pressed).

Green Mayonnaise

This dressing makes a good dip for fresh, raw vegetable relishes. It is also delicious with chicken or turkey.

3   egg yolks
3   tablespoons white wine vinegar
⅔   cup lightly packed chopped fresh parsley
¼   cup sliced green onions
¾   teaspoon *each* salt and dry mustard
⅛   teaspoon dried tarragon
¼   cup olive oil
1   cup salad oil

1. In blender container or food processor (with metal blade) combine egg yolks, vinegar, parsley, green onions, salt, dry mustard, and tarragon.

2. Cover and turn on blender or food processor. *Immediately* begin pouring in the oil in a very slow, steady stream. Whirl or process until thick and smooth.

Makes about 2 cups.

Green Goddess Dressing

A savory complement to green or seafood salads is this colorful anchovy-accented dressing made in the manner of a blender mayonnaise. Created in San Francisco, it was named after a play popular at the time.

- 1 egg yolk
- 2 tablespoons white wine vinegar
- 1½ teaspoons lemon juice
- ¼ teaspoon salt
- 1 teaspoon *each* dried tarragon and Dijon mustard
- 6 to 8 flat anchovy fillets (about half of a 2-oz can), chopped
- 1 small clove garlic, minced or pressed
- 2 green onions, sliced
- ½ cup lightly packed chopped fresh parsley
- ⅓ cup *each* olive oil and salad oil
- ½ cup sour cream

1. In blender or food processor (with metal blade) combine egg yolk, 1 tablespoon of the vinegar, lemon juice, salt, tarragon, mustard, anchovies, garlic, green onions, and parsley.

2. Cover and turn on blender or food processor. *Immediately* begin pouring in olive oil, then salad oil, in a slow, steady steam. Whirl or process until thick and smooth.

3. Add the remaining 1 tablespoon vinegar and sour cream and blend just a few seconds, until well combined.

Makes about 1⅔ cups.

Thousand Island Dressing

The vegetable ingredients that add texture to this creamy dressing are fair game for improvisation. In place of olives and pickles you might use finely chopped sweet red or green bell pepper, pimiento, parsley, or green onions.

- 1 cup mayonnaise (or ½ cup *each* mayonnaise and sour cream)
- ¼ cup chili sauce
- 1 tablespoon *each* lemon juice and grated onion
  Pinch cayenne pepper
- 1 hard-cooked egg, shredded
- ⅓ cup finely chopped stuffed olives
- ¼ cup finely chopped sweet pickles

1. Mix mayonnaise, chili sauce, lemon juice, onion, and cayenne until smooth.

2. Mix in egg, olives, and pickles. Cover and refrigerate for 1 to 3 hours to blend flavors.

Makes about 1¾ cups.

Buttermilk Blue Cheese Dressing

This tangy dressing has a relatively low calorie count—about 50 calories per tablespoon if made with genuine mayonnaise, about 35 if you use prepared imitation mayonnaise. It is delicious with many salads.

- ½ cup mayonnaise
- 1 tablespoon chopped fresh parsley
- 1 green onion, thinly sliced
- ⅛ teaspoon *each* dried basil, oregano, rosemary, and marjoram
- 1 small clove garlic, minced or pressed
- ⅓ cup buttermilk
  Salt and pepper
- ¼ cup crumbled blue-veined cheese

1. Into mayonnaise in a medium bowl blend parsley, green onion, herbs, and garlic.

2. Using a whisk, gradually mix in buttermilk, beating until smooth and well combined. Add salt and pepper to taste. Mix in cheese. Cover and refrigerate to blend flavors (1 to 3 hours). (Dressing will keep in refrigerator up to 1 week.)

Makes about 1¼ cups.

Blue Cheese Dressing

When you make a green salad to team with this dressing, include some thinly shredded red cabbage.

- ½ cup *each* mayonnaise and sour cream
- 2 tablespoons lemon juice
- ¼ teaspoon salt
- ⅛ teaspoon seasoned pepper
- 2 green onions, thinly sliced
- ½ cup crumbled blue-veined cheese

1. Mix mayonnaise, sour cream, lemon juice, salt, and pepper until smooth.

2. Mix in onions and cheese. Cover and refrigerate for 1 to 3 hours to blend flavors.

Makes about 1⅔ cups.

Low-Calorie Cottage Cheese Dressing

Calorie counters often avoid salad dressing, because the oils that make up about 75 percent of every dressing account for about 125 calories per tablespoon. Here is a savory creamy dressing with a much lower calorie count — about 12 per tablespoon.

To this foundation dressing you can add such good-tasting but low-calorie flavorings as Dijon mustard, horseradish, and garlic. The dressing enhances either greens or seafood.

- ½ cup low-fat cottage cheese
- 1 tablespoon *each* lemon juice and fluid nonfat milk
- ½ teaspoon tarragon wine vinegar
- ⅛ teaspoon *each* salt and dried dill weed
  Pinch seasoned pepper
- 1 green onion, thinly sliced

1. In food processor or blender combine cottage cheese, lemon juice, milk, vinegar, salt, dill weed, and pepper. Cover and process or whirl until smooth and creamy.

2. Add green onion and whirl or process until mixed in well.

Makes about ⅔ cup.

Salad Bar

Dill Dressing (see page 89)

*Thousand Island Dressing
(see page 91)*

Blue Cheese Dressing (see page 91)

Carrot-Walnut Bread   Butter

*Creamy Raspberry-Glazed
Cheesecake*

Carafe Red and White Wine

Coffee

🐜 Salad Bar Buffet

This flexible party idea is borrowed from a successful restaurant format. It was inspired by the observation that many people enjoy making a meal entirely from the salad bar.

The central ingredient is an enormous bowl of mixed greens — surrounded by a variety of flavorful toppings and a choice of 3 dressings. Plan on about 2 cups of greens per person and a total of ½ to 1 cup of meats, fish, poultry, and cheese. (Good choices include drained, flaked tuna; strips of dry salami or ham; tiny peeled, cooked shrimp; shredded chicken or turkey; julienne Swiss or Cheddar cheese).

Choose vegetable add-ons from this list: sprouts (see page 21), cooked kidney and garbanzo beans, well-drained julienne beets, thinly sliced carrots, slivered red and green onions, thinly sliced cucumbers, halved cherry tomatoes, and slivered sweet red and green bell peppers. Complete the table arrangement with a bowl of homemade croutons (see page 26) and a big pepper grinder.

Creamy Raspberry-Glazed Cheesecake

¾ cup finely crushed graham cracker crumbs

2 tablespoons butter or margarine, melted

2 tablespoons sugar, mixed with ¼ teaspoon cinnamon

2 large packages (8 oz *each*) cream cheese, softened

¾ cup sugar

1 teaspoon *each* vanilla and grated lemon rind

3 eggs

1 cup sour cream
   Raspberry Glaze
   (recipe follows)

1. For crust, mix crumbs, melted butter, and the sugar-cinnamon mixture. Press evenly and firmly over bottom of an 8½- to 9-inch springform pan. Bake in 350°F oven until lightly browned (8 to 10 minutes). Cool.
2. Beat cream cheese until fluffy. Gradually beat in sugar; then beat in vanilla and lemon rind. Add eggs, one at a time, beating well after each addition. Blend in sour cream. Pour mixture over baked crust.
3. Bake in a 350°F oven until knife inserted near center comes out clean (50 to 60 minutes). Turn off oven and let cheesecake stand in oven with door ajar for 30 minutes. Cool.
4. Spread with Raspberry Glaze. Chill at least 3 hours or overnight.

Makes 8 to 10 servings.

Raspberry Glaze
Thaw 1 package (10 oz) frozen raspberries. Drain, reserving juice. Place juice in a small saucepan and add 2 tablespoons sugar, 1 tablespoon cornstarch, and about half of the berries. Bring to boiling, stirring, and cook until thickened and clear. Strain to remove seeds. To strained sauce add 2 teaspoons framboise or kirsch (clear raspberry or cherry brandy) and reserved berries. Cool to room temperature.

Carrot-Walnut Bread

3 cups unbleached all-purpose flour

1 teaspoon *each* salt and baking soda

2 teaspoons pumpkin pie spice

½ teaspoon baking powder

1 cup chopped walnuts

3 eggs

1 cup packed brown sugar

½ cup granulated sugar

1 cup salad oil

1 teaspoon vanilla

1 tablespoon grated orange rind

2 cups shredded carrots (about 4 medium)

1. In a large bowl mix flour, salt, soda, pumpkin pie spice, baking powder, and walnuts.
2. Beat eggs in a medium bowl until blended; then beat in sugars and oil until sugars dissolve. Mix in vanilla, orange rind, and carrots. Make a well in center of flour mixture, add egg mixture all at once, and stir just until evenly moistened. (Batter will be thick.)
3. Divide batter evenly into 2 greased, lightly floured 4½- by 8½-inch loaf pans.
4. Bake in a 350°F oven until loaves are well browned and a wooden pick inserted in center of each comes out clean (45 to 50 minutes). Let stand 10 minutes; then turn out onto wire racks to cool completely. Flavor is best if, after cooling, loaves are wrapped and allowed to stand at least 1 day.

Makes 2 loaves.

An easy and economical way to entertain a crowd for lunch or supper is with a well-stocked salad bar. Find the biggest bowl available and fill it with freshly torn mixed greens. Then offer three favorite dressings (we chose a dilled vinaigrette, creamy Thousand Island, and a robust blue cheese) and a variety of toppings. Moist, homemade carrot bread and a crock of sweet butter complete the main course. Dessert can be a lavish cheesecake shimmering with a raspberry glaze. Carafe red and white wines and a rich, strong coffee complete a meal that will leave everyone satisfied!

Vinegar Variety

Not very long ago it seemed there were no more than two kinds of vinegar: white and cider. For better or worse, the subject of vinegar has become more complex, and therefore much more interesting.

Vinegars vary in strength of acidity; most are 5 percent (50 grain). This measurement is usually listed on the label. If higher than 5 percent, use less vinegar than the amount called for in the recipe, tasting the dressing and adjusting for flavor.

Distilled white vinegar lacks the distinctive flavor of other vinegars. It is more often the choice for pickling than for making salad dressings. *Apple cider vinegar* has a pungent flavor and is a good choice for dressing a salad including tomatoes.

Malt vinegar, with its assertive nutlike flavor and caramel color, is favored by lovers of fish and chips and can also be used in salads when a bold flavor is desired.

Wine vinegars (white, red, or even rosé) are a good all-purpose choice for salad-making. In general, use white wine vinegar in mayonnaise, red in a vinaigrette. Recently some elegant vinegars, much esteemed in *nouvelle cuisine* salads, have been arriving from France. They are costly but often exquisite. Look for *Champagne vinegar,* or white wine vinegars infused with such fruits as raspberries *(framboises),* blueberries *(myrtilles),* cherries *(cerises),* and strawberries *(fraises).*

Sherry wine vinegar boasts a bold, nutlike flavor. Its acidity may be as great as 7 percent, so it can be used with a light hand.

Rice wine vinegar, by contrast, is milder, less than 5 percent acidity. Its gentle flavor mates well with Japanese salads and cold rice dishes.

Herb vinegars are usually an infusion of herbs in white wine vinegar. Most familiar is *tarragon wine vinegar,* but you may also come upon such ready-made flavors as thyme, garlic, shallot, sage, *poivre vert* (fresh green peppercorns), and oregano—or combinations.

Balsamic vinegar comes from Modena, Italy, and is aged in wooden barrels. This process gives it a rich, dark color and a heady flavor. It is more intense and complex than most vinegars and also somewhat higher in acidity (at least 6 percent). It can be ordered from:

Williams-Sonoma
Mail Order Department
Box 3792
San Francisco, California 94119

A Salad Oil Sampler

Vegetable oils, such as corn oil, safflower oil, peanut oil, sunflower oil, and the oils of soybeans and cottonseeds, are all light and delicate in consistency and flavor. Use them in dressings when you want a neutral flavor.

Olive oil varies in color from a distinct green to greenish golden. Its flavor may be fresh and fruity or fairly strong. Spanish and Greek olive oils tend to have stronger flavors than those from Italy or the south of France. The highest quality (and most expensive) olive oils are designated as virgin oil from the first cold-pressing.

Nut oils include walnut oil (if French, *huile de noix*), filbert or hazelnut oil *(huile de noisette),* and almond oil. All taste distinctly of the nuts from which they are pressed and can add intriguing flavors to green salads. Of the three, almond oil is the mildest in flavor. Look for them in stores specializing in French foods and in natural foods stores.

Sesame oil: The Oriental variety, pressed from toasted seeds, has so much flavor it is usually used only a teaspoon at a time to season Chinese and Japanese dishes. That found in natural foods stores is much blander and cannot be used interchangeably with the Oriental kind.

Index